Prosocial Rule-Breakers and the Law

Ova Cummerata

TABLE OF CONENTS

DEDICATION iii

ACKNOWLEDGEMENTS iv

LIST OF TABLES viii

LIST OF FIGURES xi

ABSTRACT.. xii

CHAPTER	PAGE

INTRODUCTION 1

I. PROSOCIAL RULE-BREAKING...5

    Prosocial Rule-Breaking and Antisocial Rule-Breaking 5

    Predicting Prosocial Rule-Breaking 8

II. LEGAL SOCIALIZATION 10

    Internal and External Factors 10

    Moral Reasoning 11

    Legal Reasoning 13

    Moral Reasoning versus Moral Heuristics..14

    The Integrated Cognitive Legal Socialization Model..17

    The Procedural Justice Legal Socialization Model...19

III. GAPS TO ADDRESS..24

    The Measurement of Moral and Legal Reasoning..24

    No Measure of Prosocial Rule-Violating Behavior 27

    Present Studies..28

IV. STUDY 1: DEVELOPMENT OF THE LAMAS SCALE 29

    Method 30

    Results 35

    Discussion 43

V. STUDY 2: EXPERIMENTAL TEST OF PREDICTIVE DIFFERENCES 45

    Method 46

    Results 50

    Discussion 59

VI. STUDY 3 LONGITUDINAL DEVELOPMENT 63

    Method 64

    Results 68

    Discussion 72

VII. GENERAL DISCUSSION 74

    Key Findings 75

    Implications 77

    Limitations and Future Directions 82

    Conclusions 84

LIST OF REFERENCES 86

APPENDIX A: PROPOSED DEONTOLOGICAL MORAL AND LEGAL REASONING ITEMS 110

APPENDIX B: PROSOCIAL AND ANTISOCIAL RULE-VIOLATING BEHAVIOR ITEMS 112

SCALE 114

ABSTRACT

Legal socialization research is the backbone of many educational, forensic, and intervention programs aiming to prevent criminal behavior, yet researchers in this field and other disciplines define rule-breaking exclusively as harmful/antisocial behavior. This classification fails to explain rule-breaking motivated by prosocial intentions (e.g., clashing with police over racial injustice, hiding Jewish families during Nazi Germany, and violating racial segregation laws during the civil rights movement). The studies described here intend to adapt two legal socialization models so they clearly distinguish prosocial rule-breaking from antisocial rule-breaking. Across three studies, I present findings that validate the distinction between morality and legality, identify external social and internal moral factors that motivate prosocial rule-breaking as opposed to antisocial rule-breaking, and determine the developmental differences between prosocial and antisocial rule-breaking using the two predominant legal socialization models. In Study 1, I developed a novel scale measuring the two factors of moral and legal alignment. In Study 2, I also further validate the moral and legal alignment scale and demonstrate the predictive ability of its two factors when expanding the integrated cognitive model of legal socialization. Study 2 employs a cross-sectional within-subjects experimental design to determine differences between prosocial and antisocial rule-breaking in how they are predicted by the integrated model and the procedural justice model of legal socialization. In Study 3, I examine the development of prosocial rule-breaking using both the integrated cognitive model and procedural justice model in a longitudinal design across three waves. This research helps dispel the myth that all rule-breakers are antisocial, giving researchers, forensic investigators, judges, and juries greater clarity in understanding the moral motivations behind the rule-breaking perennially at the forefront of positive social change.

INTRODUCTION

In an open letter written from his cell in Birmingham County Jail, Martin Luther King Jr. challenged his fellow clergymen's praise of the Birmingham police for arresting peaceful protesters. He wrote, "One has not only a legal but a moral responsibility to obey just laws. Conversely, one has a moral responsibility to disobey unjust laws" (1963). This sentiment explained his rationale for disobeying a blanket injunction that prohibited civil demonstrations for racial equality deliberately. King was jailed for actively trying to improve society and help others. He broke the law to promote social acceptance and human rights for all. By all definitions, he was engaging in prosocial behavior (Batson & Powell, 2003; Baumsteiger & Siegal, 2019). Yet, this overlap between prosocial and illegal behavior is poorly understood. Psychologists, criminologists, and legal socialization researchers define breaking the law as antisocial behavior (e.g., Raine & Yang, 2006). Legal socialization researchers fail to investigate or acknowledge the development of prosocial rule-breaking – the act of breaking the rules to help others (Hennigan & Cohn, 2022). Examining the internal conflict between morality and legality and the environmental influences that shape this behavior may help explain a range of important behavior ranging from civil disobedience to misguided terrorism. The purpose of my dissertation is to address this gap and examine the developmental factors that lead to prosocial rule-breaking by applying the two dominant legal socialization models.

Legal socialization refers to the normative process through which individuals come to acquire societal values and beliefs related to legal rules, legal authorities, and legal institutions (Cohn & White, 1990; Fine & Trinkner, 2020; Grant, 2006; Levine, 1979; Tapp, 1976; Levine & Tapp, 1977; Tapp & Kohlberg, 1977). These values and beliefs about the legal sphere are instrumental to the development of rule-violating behavior and, consequentially, legal socialization research serves as the foundation of many educational, forensic, and intervention programs designed to curtail criminal behavior (e.g., Cauffman et al., 2021; Heidary et al., 2021; Mazerolle et al., 2021). Yet, despite calls from moral psychologists to avoid the practice of comparing moral judgements to established normative standards (Holyoak & Powell, 2016), researchers in this field continue to define rule-breaking exclusively as antisocial (harmful) behavior (e.g., Coie & Dodge, 1998; Fagan & Tyler, 2005; Mazerolle et al., 2021; Raine & Yang, 2006) and as antithetical to prosocial (helpful) behavior (Batson & Powell, 2003; Baumsteiger & Siegal, 2019). Within this framework, rule-breaking is considered an impulsive, self-interested act that is harmful to others (De Wall et al., 2011; Gottfredson & Hirschi, 1990; Nogami & Yoshida, 2013). As a result, the intervention programs that rely on legal socialization models are all designed to actively suppress every type of rule-breaking, regardless of if it is helpful or harmful (Baek et al., 2020; Cheon et al, 2018). The problem seems to arise from researchers taking the same normative stance as the law itself – that breaking the law is always harmful to society.

In his quote, King understood that adherence to legal rules and moral rules are not necessarily one and the same. While they often do overlap, it is important that researchers and intervention programs distinguish between the two. We rely on research-informed programs to encourage positive development in children and adolescents through socialization processes (e.g., Heidary et al., 2021), with some of the most prevalent relying on legal socialization models (e.g., Cauffman et al., 2021; Fine et al., 2019). When prosocial rule-breaking is incorrectly labelled as antisocial, these programs may inadvertently suppress the often illegal moral behavior at the forefront of positive social change while simultaneously justifying its punishment with harsh sanctions intended for antisocial behavior. Because prosocial rule-breaking is often the first step in changing outdated and unjust laws and harmful social norms, it is critical that we understand how it differs from antisocial behavior and how and why it arises.

Understanding prosocially motivated rule-breaking may also explain the devastating actions of terrorists and could also serve as a means of curbing such behavior. Because of the wide-spread societal harm caused by their acts, terrorists are assumed to have antisocial intent (Victoroff, 2005). Yet, researchers have found a surprising lack of antisocial characteristics in terrorists (Horgan, 2005; Victoroff, 2005). Counterintuitively, empirical evidence suggests terrorists are motivated by prosocial inclinations towards their own social group which may be at odds with the social norms of the wider society at large (della Porta, 1988; Pedahzur et al., 2003). For example, members of the Provisional Irish Republican Army (PIRA) have bombed military and political targets of the established authority with the prosocial intent of restoring all of Ireland to independent rule. This is of course at odds with the established laws of the Republic of Ireland and the United Kingdom who both designate PIRA as a terrorist organization (Oppenheimer, 2008). Similarly, the psychological motivations behind many suicide bombers may be altruistic, with the prosocial goal of benefiting their religious organization at the personal sacrifice of their own life (Pedahzur et al., 2003). Despite the harmful consequences of terrorism, it is important to investigate the possible prosocial intent underlying the psychology of a terrorist. By falsely assuming all terrorism is driven by antisocial intent, we may fail to recognize morally motivated terrorists and intervene before they harm others.

Whether the consequences are harmful or helpful, it is important to model the development of prosocial rule-breaking. Current legal socialization models may predict prosocial rule-breaking differently than antisocial rule-breaking leading to misclassification of individuals in risk-assessments, forensic investigations, and intervention programs. Prosocial behaviors that are helpful to society such as the civil disobedience carried out by civil rights activists may be inadvertently suppressed while potential terrorists may elude investigators and risk-assessments leading to mass societal harm. We need to determine if prosocially motivated rule-breaking is in fact motivated by the same legal and moral inclinations that drive other types of prosocial behavior rather than blindly applying models that predict antisocial rule-breaking. These are the goals of this dissertation.

Across three studies, I present findings that further validate the distinction between morality and legality, identify social and internal factors that motivate prosocial rule-breaking as opposed to antisocial rule-breaking, and determine developmental differences between prosocial and antisocial rule-breaking using the two predominant legal socialization models. In Study 1, I developed a novel scale measuring the two factors of moral and legal alignment. This was done to better distinguish morality from legality in order to accurately predict the differences between prosocial and antisocial rule-breaking. In Study 2, I further validate the moral and legal alignment scale and demonstrate the predictive capacity of its two factors in the integrated cognitive model of legal socialization using a cross-sectional design (Cohn et al., 2010). Study 2 also employs a within-subjects experimental design to determine differences between prosocial and antisocial rule-violating behavior in how they are predicted by the integrated model and the procedural justice model of legal socialization. Study 3 examines the development of prosocial rule-breaking using both the integrated cognitive model and procedural justice model in a longitudinal design.

CHAPTER I

PROSOCIAL RULE-BREAKING

Prosocial Rule-Breaking and Antisocial Rule-Breaking as Separate Concepts

Prosocial behavior is any helpful act intended to benefit others (Batson & Powell, 2003; Dovidio et al., 2017), while rule-breaking is generally understood as harmful antisocial behavior such as juvenile delinquency and adult criminal behavior (American Psychiatric Association, 2013; Patterson et al., 1989). Seemingly oxymoronic, prosocial rule-breaking is the violation of any institutional rule with the intended goal of helping others (Hennigan & Cohn, 2022). While it is possible that prosocial rule-breaking can cause harm in pursuit of helping others (e.g., speeding to get a friend to the hospital can still cause an accident), it is typically defined by its intent and internal moral motivations rather than its ultimate consequences.

Confusingly, whereas prosocial behavior is most often defined by its intent (Batson & Powell, 2003), antisocial behavior is often defined by its consequences (e.g., Raine & Yang, 2006). Antisocial behavior is any hostile or aggressive act that harms others (Coie & Dodge, 1998; Walker et al., 2004). As such, antisocial rule-breaking is the exclusively harmful rule-breaking typically studied and understood by psychologists, criminologists, and legal scholars. It is rare that individuals engage in antisocial behavior with the intended goal of harming others. More often, the harm comes as a side effect of some intended goal to selfishly benefit oneself without regard for other's welfare (Koolen et al., 2012; van Leeuwen et al., 2014). Antisocial rule-breaking is distinguished from prosocial rule-breaking in that the intended goal is to benefit oneself instead of others and is facilitated by a lack of internal moral motivations (Halali et al.,

2014; Kahane et al., 2015). In short, antisocial rule-breaking is the violation of any institutional rule with the intended goal of personal gain without regard for the welfare of others (Hennigan & Cohn, 2022).

Although research on prosocial rule-breaking is extremely limited due to its very recent conceptualization, research investigating general prosocial behavior is consistent with the definition described above. For example, general prosocial behavior is *positively* associated with empathy (Batson, 2011; Batson et al., 1981; Morelli et al., 2015), proneness to feel moral emotions such as guilt (Caprara et al., 2001; Malti & Krettenauer, 2013; Quiles & Bybee, 1997), and prosocial intentions (Baumsteiger & Siegal, 2019). This differs from antisocial rule-breaking which is *negatively* associated with empathy (Jolliffe & Farrington, 2004; Miller & Eisenberg, 1988), guilt-proneness (Cole et al., 2014; Cole et al., 2021; Rebellon et al., 2016; Stuewig et al., 2015), and prosocial intentions (Chouhy et al., 2017). Unsurprisingly, trait empathy, guilt-proneness, and moral identity consistently correlate with each other across studies (e.g., Hennigan & Cohn, 2022) resembling a general overarching sense of prosocial concern.

The reason these moral characteristics associate with prosocial and antisocial behavior in opposite directions is well understood. For example, empathy allows one to feel what others are feeling and highly empathic individuals are motivated to engage in prosocial behavior to promote shared positive affect and they avoid antisocial behavior to reduce shared distress (Morelli et al., 2015). Individuals with low empathy have little internal psychological motivation to avoid antisocial behavior so their self-interest takes precedence (Miller & Eisenberg, 1988). Guilt-prone individuals are likely to anticipate the aversive feelings of guilt associated with antisocial behavior, so they avoid acting antisocially and engage in prosocial behavior to avoid feeling this way (Cole et al., 2014, 2021; Tangney, Stuewig, & Mashek, 2007b). People with a strong internal moral identity help others and avoid harming them because of their self-concept as a morally good person, while people with a strong symbolic moral identity engage in helpful moral behavior and avoid antisocial behavior to signal to others that they are consistent with the social norms of their group identity (Aquino & Reed, 2002).

While some instances of observable prosocial behavior can be self-interested, such as when a self-interested person strategically helps with the intended goal of receiving something in return, research supports the existence of "true" prosocial behavior driven by prosocial intentions (Batson, 2018). This behavior is driven by first-order implicit concern for others with deliberate self-interest being absent or existing outside of conscious awareness (Bartels & Pizarro, 2011; Crockett et al., 2010; Glenn et al., 2010; Halali et al., 2014; Kahane et al., 2015; Rand, 2016; Rand et al., 2012; Wiech et al., 2013). Conversely, deliberate self-interest has been identified as a critical cognitive component that underlies antisocial behavior and antisocial rule-breaking (Barriga & Gibbs, 1996; van Leeuwen et al., 2014; Raine & Uh, 2018; Wallinius et al., 2011).

Those with higher levels of prosocial concern (trait empathy, guilt-proneness, and internal moral identity) engage in higher levels of moral reasoning. In short, these underlying moral characteristics become incorporated as a factor in one's cognitive logic when making moral decisions (Blair, 1995; Koenigs et al., 2007; Valdesolo & DeSteno, 2006). When reasoning about moral dilemmas, one's prosocial concern becomes a factor that adds weight to moral decisions, increasing the likelihood of prosocial behavior. Without prosocial concern to inform their cognitive logic, individuals become more likely to engage in antisocial behavior.

Because prosocial rule-breaking and antisocial rule-breaking have the potential to cause harm and typically involve going against the norms of society, it is easy to see how they have been considered one and the same by psychologists and criminologists for so long. To disentangle the two and separate them into prosocial and antisocial categories for the sake of studying them in a psychological context, it makes more sense to focus on internal prosocial concern rather than external consequences such as potential for harm. This focus on the psychological motivations rather than normative standards is consistent with calls from moral psychologists to resist comparing moral judgements to our own favored normative standards (Holyoak & Powell, 2016).

Predicting Prosocial Rule-Breaking

When outlining his *social concern theory* of crime, criminological theorist Agnew (2014) suggested the possibility that prosocial concern can sometimes increase rule-breaking. Despite this mention, researchers have not investigated this possibility until very recently (Hennigan & Cohn, 2022). To connect the literature linking prosocial intentions, empathy, and guilt-proneness with prosocial behavior directly to prosocial rule-breaking, Hennigan and Cohn (2022) developed a self-report scale that measures perceived likelihood to engage in either prosocial or antisocial rule-breaking. This self-report scale measures how likely participants would be to engage in a series of hypothetical behaviors across a range of moral dilemmas where the behavior described is to break a formal legal or informal non-legal rule. In half of these scenarios, the reason for breaking the rule is to help others (prosocial rule-breaking) and in the remaining half, the reason for breaking the rule is a benefit only to the rule breaker (antisocial rule-breaking).

Consistent with Agnew's (2014) theoretical claims, the results linked prosocial intentions, empathy, and guilt-proneness positively to prosocial rule-breaking, providing the first evidence that prosocial rule-breaking is connected to the same prosocial concern that underlies prosocial rule-following behavior. The antisocial rule-breaking component of the scale was negatively associated with these same factors, indicating its association with a lack of prosocial concern. These findings were consistent with a history of researchers investigating the factors underlying antisocial rule-breaking (e.g., Chouhy et al., 2017; Cole et al., 2014; Cole et al., 2021; Jolliffe & Farrington, 2004; Miller & Eisenberg, 1988; Rebellon et al., 2016; Stuewig et al., 2015). These results showed that prosocial rule-breaking was not synonymous with antisocial behavior, but was better understood as a type of prosocial behavior as it had the same underlying moral characteristics and prosocial concern that underlie other types of prosocial behavior (Hennigan & Cohn, 2022). Furthermore, for each one-point increase on a scale ranging from 1 to 7, the prosocial rule-breaking measure predicted a 268% increase in actual cheating behavior when it helps others but not when it only helps oneself. The prosocial rule-breaking measure also predicted a 37% increase in likelihood to participate in the summer protests of 2020 while the antisocial rule-breaking factor had no relation to protest behavior. These results provided the first evidence of the prosocial rule-breaking scale's predictive validity.

While these results revealed the existence of prosocial rule-breaking as fundamentally different from antisocial rule-breaking, it must be integrated into existing developmental models before it can have practical benefits. Furthermore, it would be beneficial to investigate the development of actual prosocial rule-violating behavior in addition to perceived likelihood of engaging in prosocial rule-breaking. Before we can inform educators and intervention programs on how to best reduce harmful antisocial rule-breaking while preserving helpful prosocial rule-breaking, we must understand what developmental factors lead one to become a prosocial rule-breaker as opposed to an antisocial rule-breaker. This can be accomplished by incorporating prosocial rule-breaking into the widely used legal socialization framework.

CHAPTER II

LEGAL SOCIALIZATION

Internal and External Factors

Prosocial rule-breaking is a complex behavior driven by internal psychological factors such as guilt-proneness and empathy, but like all rule-violating behavior, it should also be influenced by external social factors such as prior interactions with authorities and the social norms of their time. Researchers interested in explaining and preventing antisocial rule-breaking often look at internal factors such as the development of our ability to reason about morality and legality, but also by examining external developmental factors such as how one is socialized to perceive authority and legal rules (Cohn & White, 1990; Trinkner & Cohn, 2014). Legal socialization research necessarily investigates both.

Legal socialization refers to the process through which individuals come to understand legal rules and their relationship with legal authorities and the law (Cohn et al., 2010; Cohn & White, 1990; Fagan & Piquero, 2007; Fagan & Tyler, 2005; Fine & Trinkner, 2020; Piquero, et al., 2005). This process involves acquiring beliefs about the law and rule-breaking by internalizing codified social norms (Levine & Tapp, 1977; Tapp, 1976; Tapp & Kohlberg, 1977). Legal socialization occurs through the influence of external social factors such as interactions with police officers and other authority figures (Fagan & Tyler, 2005; Fagan & Piquero, 2007; Piquero et al., 2005; Trinkner & Cohn, 2014; Tyler & Trinkner, 2017) as well as through the influence of internal psychological factors such as the development of one's cognitive reasoning ability (Cohn & White, 1990; Cohn et al., 2010).

On the external level, our sense of legality is shaped through the social influence of others throughout the lifespan, instilling in people the social norms of whichever society they belong. This includes learning the laws and informal rules specific to one's culture and developing a conception of rule adherence and rule violation (Levine & Tapp, 1977; Tapp, 1976; Tapp & Levine, 1974; Trinkner & Cohn, 2014; Tyler & Trinkner, 2017). On the internal level, our sense of morality is supplemented by our developing reasoning ability allowing more complex moral judgements (Kohlberg, 1971; Tapp & Kohlberg, 1971). Furthermore, our internal reasoning capacity also allows for more complex judgements about the codified social norms acquired from external sources. These two developing abilities – moral reasoning and legal reasoning are integrated through the process of legal socialization resulting in individual differences in rule-violating behavior (Cohn & White, 1990; Cohn et al., 2010).

Moral Reasoning

Theories of moral reasoning and legal socialization have a shared history as they both grew from the classic work of Kohlberg and his proposed stages of moral development (1971). Kohlberg subscribed to Kant's (1785) approach to morals, where morality was believed to be a purely rational process (1785). He proposed that children make increasingly sophisticated and complex judgements about right and wrong as they grow older and refine this skill much like a practiced philosopher would (Kohlberg, 1968). With age, they are proposed to develop better moral reasoning by progressing through a series of linear stages so they can make more advanced judgments about whether a behavior is moral or immoral (Kohlberg, 1963; Tapp & Kohlberg, 1971).

In Kohlberg's (1963; 1971) framework, children begin in the preconventional moral reasoning stage and only follow rules to avoid punishment selfishly and receive rewards for good behavior. As their capacity for moral reasoning increases, they soon progress into the conventional stage and place value on the rules themselves and embrace conformity with the belief that adherence to social norms is best for society as a whole. Finally, those with the most advanced moral reasoning progress into the post-conventional stage where they develop an advanced abstract conception of morality and adhere to rationally derived moral rules that take precedence over norms and legal rules. Those with a post-conventional ability to morally reason are rare and can make judgements deduced from abstract universal moral principles, adhere to logical comprehensiveness, and have the advanced philosophical ability to determine which laws are unjust, and to change, or create new laws According to proponents of this theory, individuals are less likely to break laws as they improve their moral reasoning skills, despite the value of moral principles eventually overtaking that of legal principles.

Past researchers appear to support this negative relation between moral reasoning and rule-violating behavior (Blasi, 1980; Matsueda, 1989; Palmer, 2003). For example, Hains and Miller (1980) found that delinquents had lower moral reasoning levels than non-delinquents. This negative relation between moral reasoning and rule-violation appears to remain stable over time (Raaijmakers, Engels, & Van Hoof, 2005), is supported by a meta-analysis (Stams et al., 2006), and appears stronger for males (Palmer & Hollin, 2001). However, these researchers vary greatly in how they operationally define "moral" reasoning. For example, Palmer and Hollin (2001) employ the Sociomoral Reflection Measure (Gibbs et al., 1992) which aims to measure how much one values the five norms of contract and truth, affiliation, life, property and law. Legal justice with the focus on legal values, conformity, and adherence differ from Kohlberg's idea of morality eventually transcending legality as moral reasoning progresses to its highest stage.

Legal Reasoning

The first distinction between morality and legality in the legal socialization literature appeared as theorists introduced another cognitive developmental factor: legal reasoning (Tapp & Kohlberg, 1971; Tapp & Levine, 1974). In many ways, legal reasoning parallels moral reasoning in that it follows a stage-like progression of development. However, while moral reasoning is ultimately concerned with universal moral principles that are independent of social norms and the law, legal reasoning focuses specifically on judgments about laws established by society's legal institutions. Legal reasoning helps define, interpret, and make decisions about laws, rights, and responsibilities (Levine & Tapp, 1977; Tapp & Levine, 1974). A person's ability to reason about legal issues influences whether they accept or reject a law, reform or maintain a law, and if they decide to break or follow that law. Like moral reasoning, as people develop higher legal reasoning skills, they are less likely to violate and more likely to comply with laws. Though research on this relationship is less extensive compared to moral reasoning and rule-violation, it does support a negative association between legal reasoning and rule-violating behavior (Cohn et al., 2010; Cohn & White, 1990). This link seems valid across several cultures, being found in U.S. undergraduates (Cohn & White, 1990), Russian adolescents (Finckenauer, 1995), and Mexican youth (Grant, 2006).

Researchers later suggested that the relation between legal reasoning and rule-violation was more complex (Cohn & White, 1990). Rather than legal reasoning directly influencing rule-violating behavior, they concluded that this relation was mediated by attitudes towards rule-violating (Cohn et al., 2010). Cohn and White identified two main attitudes in this process: normative status and enforcement status. Normative status referred to individuals' approval of rule-violating behavior, while enforcement status centered on people's beliefs that rule-violating behavior should be appropriately punished. In their study of undergraduates, they found that higher legal reasoning indeed predicted less approval of rule-violating behavior and stronger beliefs that such behavior should be punished, which subsequently influenced reduced engagement in rule-violating behavior. This same relation was later supported in a longitudinal examination of middle school and high school students. However, there remains debate on how to accurately measure reasoning, with the original studies originally using Tapp's conception of legal reasoning rooted in the tradition of Kohlberg (Cohn et al., 2010; Tapp & Kohlberg, 1971; Tapp & Levine, 1974) before switching to a measure of everyday legal reasoning which is more grounded in everyday experiences as measured by perceived likelihood to violate or adhere to a variety of rules presented in hypothetical scenarios (Cohn et al, 2012).

Moral Reasoning versus Moral Heuristics

There are several theoretical approaches to explain the reasoning process with more recent theories challenging the classic work of Kohlberg and Tapp (Kohlberg,1963; Tapp & Kohlberg, 1971). In particular, Kohlberg's idea that moral reasoning is a deliberate cognitive process that progresses in stages resembling the growth of a practiced philosopher may not be as accurate as once assumed. At first glance, this original theory seems to be a good candidate for predicting the development of prosocial rule-breaking. Prosocial rule-breaking may seem to be the obvious product of post-conventional moral reasoning due to the appearance of moral rules taking precedence over legal rules. If this were true, prosocial rule-breaking would be the rational result of the most advanced stage of moral reasoning. However, a closer investigation reveals that this is unlikely to explain most instances of prosocial rule-breaking.

Kohlberg argued that moral judgments were rational choices based on deliberate reasoning and that these advanced processes were required to overcome the innate self-interest intrinsic to humanity (1984). Only after sufficiently developing our rational capacity could we overcome this limitation and such development may require many years of cognitive development before a person could achieve post-conventional reasoning, if they are able to achieve it at all (Kohlberg; 1984). The surprising reality is that the moral judgments based on deliberate rational thinking lead to more selfish choices compared to the automatic intuitive choices made under strict time constraints (Crockett et al., 2010; Halali et al., 2014; Rand et al., 2012; Righetti et al., 2013). This becomes apparent when noting the recent developments in cognitive science, moral psychology, and neuroscience which cast doubt on the validity of Kohlberg's (1963, 1984) theory (see Rand, 2016 for a meta-analysis linking deliberate rational thought to selfish, antisocial choices).

These developments suggest that morality is largely an automatic default process (Greene, 2013; Greene et al., 2001; Rand et al., 2012), where we automatically feel that an action is morally wrong or right without any need for complex rational thought. This is consistent with research on empathy, where we feel what another is feeling (Batson, 2011; Batson et al., 1981; Morelli et al., 2015), emotional guilt, where we feel bad about our transgressions (Cole et al., 2014; Cole et al., 2021; Rebellon et al., 2016; Stuewig et al., 2015), and moral outrage, where we feel anger towards other people's transgressions (Crocket et al, 2017).

Such processes do not come about after years of overcoming our selfish nature by developing our ability to reason, but appear to be innately present in children as young as 1 year old, with babies as young as 3 months showing preference for those who help others and an aversion to those who harm (Bloom, 2014). The idea that we come equipped with a basic moral sense is supported by dedicated networks in the brain such as those mediated between the more rational processes of the prefrontal cortex and the quick emotional responses of the amygdala by the ventral medial prefrontal cortex (VMPFC; Greene et al., 2001; Greene, 2008). Many studies show that when the VMPFC is damaged or destroyed due to traumatic brain injury the individual loses their basic moral sense and engages in previously uncharacteristic antisocial behavior while showing a disturbing lack of prosocial concern (Damasio et al., 1994). Of course, even in otherwise healthy individuals there is variance in the strength of this basic moral sense as exemplified by psychopaths showing reduced gray matter in and around the VMPFC (Mendez, 2009). The point here is that morality as a construct exists prior to and often independently of the legal socialization processes that give us a sense of legality.

This is not to say that socialization processes are irrelevant and that we are permanently "hardwired" to only follow this basic moral sense of right (helping) and wrong (hurting). Like all psychological processes, our moral and legal judgements are a result of complex interactions between our experiences and inherited tendencies. Despite being equipped with a basic moral sense of right and wrong, arbitrary actions and beliefs can be *moralized* through socialization processes (Rhee et al., 2019), with individual belief in the moral nature of the law being a prime example. From a very early age, children begin to learn about the norms and rules particular to their culture as well as the consequences of breaking those rules.

Despite much overlap between codified legal rules and our default moral beliefs that helping is good and harming is bad, the law and morality can be at odds with each other (Holyoak & Powell, 2016; Zamir & Medina, 2010). Laws that clearly harm others without any benefit to society have certainly been implemented (e.g., those enacted by the Nazi party to facilitate the Holocaust) and helpful moral behavior has often been made illegal (e.g., helping enslaved people escape through the Underground Railroad). Yet, when people are socialized to believe that following the law is equivalent to being moral, the law itself becomes moralized and our automatic heuristics shift to accommodate these socialized beliefs (Rand et al., 2012; Rhee et al., 2019). This is not to say that reasoning does not play a role, but that the very reasons we use as guidelines for our behavior are implicitly molded by socialization processes rather than an increased capacity for philosophical rationality as first suggested by Kohlberg (1968).

The ability to distinguish morality and legality is critical to understanding the multidimensional nature of prosocial rule-breaking where the prosociality should be attached to the moral dimension while the rule-breaking should be attached to the legal dimension. Rather than considering morality and legality as a singular dimension as researchers often do, breaking them into two separate scalable factors provides the nuance needed to accurately model the development of prosocial rule-breaking. The legal socialization model that best captures this multidimensional nature is the Integrated Cognitive Legal Socialization Model.

The Integrated Cognitive Legal Socialization Model

Legal socialization models that explain illegal rule-violating behavior have since progressed beyond Kohlberg's original ideas (1963, 1974). Building from Kohlberg and Tapp's (1971) original theories, legal socialization researchers integrated moral reasoning and legal reasoning into the same model as co-occurring, but distinct processes (Cohn et al., 2010). This line of legal socialization research has culminated with the advent of the Integrated Cognitive Legal Socialization Model which shows that greater levels of moral and legal reasoning are associated with less rule-breaking and that this effect is mediated by attitudes towards the rules themselves (approval of breaking the rules, and belief that breaking the rules should be punished; Cohn et al., 2010; Cohn et al., 2012; Figure 1).
Furthermore, this model took an additional step over the original reasoning theories by focusing on everyday moral reasoning (Shelton & McAdams, 1990) and everyday legal reasoning (Cohn

Figure 1

The Integrated Cognitive Model

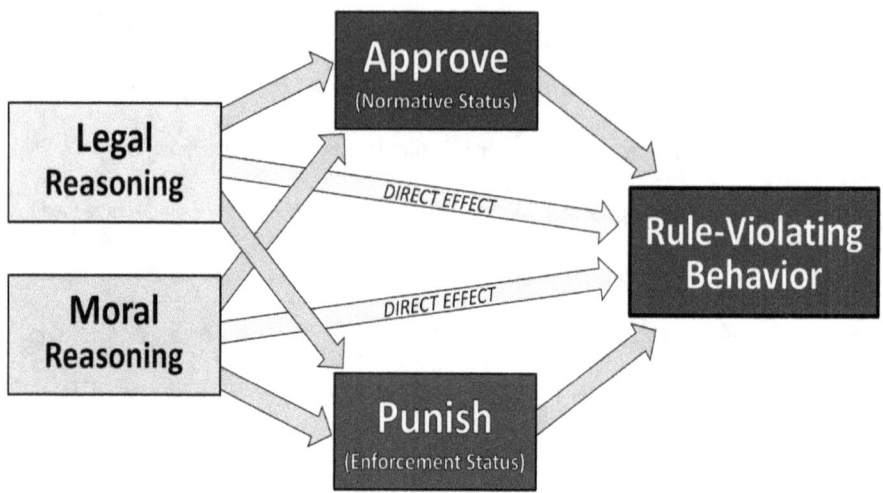

et al., 2012) rather than the abstract philosophical reasoning originally posited by Kohlberg. Due to its ability to distinguish morality from legality, the Integrated Model serves as a prime candidate for explaining the development of prosocial rule-breaking. Prosocial rule-breaking should be associated with *greater* moral reasoning and lower legal reasoning unlike antisocial rule-breaking which should be associated with *lower* moral reasoning in addition to lower legal reasoning.

Despite the Integrated Model's predictive utility in explaining antisocial rule-breaking and its prime candidacy for predicting prosocial rule-breaking, there are some limitations that should be addressed. While the everyday reasoning measures were an important step forward, they are ultimately measuring the perceived likelihood to engage in behavior as an approximation of the reasons assumed to underlie those behaviors. While the approach could theoretically capture automatic moral and legal heuristics in addition to more thought-out reasoning processes, it remains uncertain which is being measured as both could influence responses to hypothetical moral dilemmas. As such, future researchers should aim to supplement these everyday measures with new moral reasoning and legal reasoning measures that directly focus on the underlying reasons that precede these responses to moral and legal dilemmas. Furthermore, legal socialization theory assumes that our reasoning is shaped by socialization processes, but the Integrated Cognitive Model only captures the internal cognitive component without directly modelling the external socialization processes themselves.

The Procedural Justice Legal Socialization Model

The prosocial rule-breakers described in the opening pages of this dissertation share a common feature where nearly all mention they were motivated by a sense of social justice, discontent with the law, and by perceptions of authority figures as being unjust (Ellis-Petersen, 2021; O'Doherty, 2021; Parks & Haskins, 1992; Theoharis, 2015). Therefore, a model that is capable of measuring the development and socialization of justice perspectives would offer a complimentary framework for predicting prosocial rule-breaking from a strictly external socialization perspective. While the Integrated Cognitive Legal Socialization Model is concerned with the internal factors of moral and legal reasoning, the procedural justice model focuses on the external social interactions and observations of the law. It is not to say that one model supersedes the other, it is that each model focuses on the different components of internal and external influences driving the legal socialization process.

As a compliment to the integrated model, the procedural justice legal socialization model predicts rule-breaking through the changing perspectives of authorities as an individual interacts with and observes the social behavior of authorities (Fagan & Tyler, 2005; Fagan & Piquero, 2007; Piquero et al., 2005; Trinkner & Cohn, 2014; Tyler & Trinkner, 2017). The procedural justice model shows that when individuals perceive authorities as behaving in a fair manner, they are more likely to internalize the values exemplified by those authorities, perceive those authorities to be legitimate, and behave in accordance with the rules set by those authorities (Trinkner & Cohn, 2014; Trinkner et al., 2018; Tyler & Trinkner, 2017). Conversely, when authority figures are perceived as treating individuals unfairly, these individuals develop a cynicism towards the law and perceive these authorities as being illegitimate which results in a greater degree of rule-violating behavior (Figure 2).

Figure 2

The Procedural Justice Model

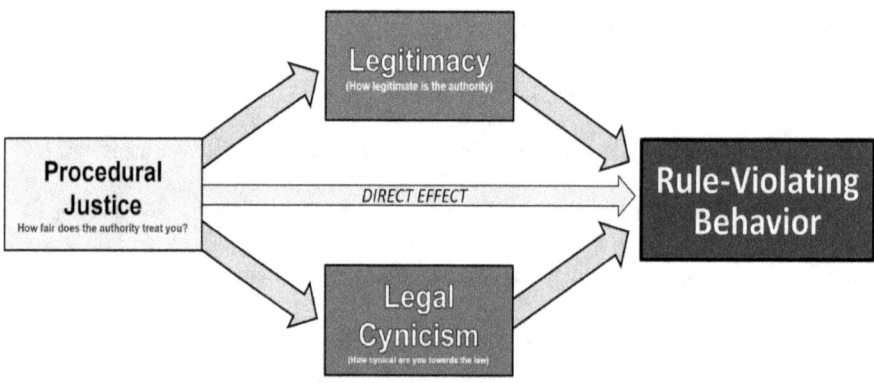

The first developmental step in the model is an individual's perception of procedural justice. Procedural justice is the perceived fairness of the procedures and processes carried about by an authority (Lind & Tyler, 1988 Trinkner & Cohn, 2014; Tyler, 1988). In short, it can be thought of as an individual's perception of how fair the authority member treats others or the individual. Procedural justice is unique in that it is focused on the procedures that lead to the decisions made by authority figures rather than the decisions themselves (Thibaut & Walker, 1975). A judgement of whether an authority acted in a fair manner is less concerned with the resulting decision made by a particular authority figure, but their perception of fairness depends on *how* that decision was made (Boldizar & Samuelson, 1985; Tyler, 2000; Tyler et al., 1997; Tyler & Lind, 1992; Trinkner & Cohn, 2014). The main elements of procedures that shape an individual's perception are whether they are given the opportunity to express their perspective (voice), whether the procedures treat everyone equally (impartiality), how they are treated by authority (respect), and whether the authority is perceived to care about those affected by their procedures and choices (benevolence; Kennealy et al., 2012; Piquero et al., 2005; Trinkner & Cohn, 2014; Tyler, 2000; Tyler & Huo, 200).

Procedural justice is theoretically relevant to prosocial rule-breaking because many prosocial rule-breakers explicitly state that the authority figures who enforce and create laws are unjust (Ellis-Petersen, 2021; O'Doherty, 2021; Parks & Haskins, 1992; Theoharis, 2015). When an individual perceives an authority figure to not be giving them voice, to be treating people unequally, as disrespectful, and uncaring, they should become incensed and the likelihood that they become a prosocial rule-breaker should be increased. In the case of prosocial rule-breakers, the caring dimension in particular may carry the most weight because prosocial rule-breakers are largely driven by feelings of empathy (Hennigan & Cohn, 2022). A perceived lack of empathy in authority figures should matter more to empathic individuals as empathy is important to those who engage in any type of prosocial behavior (Batson, 2018). A highly empathic individual witnessing a lack of empathy in an authority figure would likely perceive them as unfair due to the disparity of moral values between them and the authority figure.

This leads to the second developmental step that occurs after an individual establishes their perceptions of authority as unfair. This step is the perceived legitimacy of that authority and legal cynicism (Trinkner & Cohn, 2014; Tyler & Trinkner, 2017). Legitimacy can be thought of as one's perception of whether an authority figure has any stake to rule (Trinkner & Cohn, 2014; Tyler, 2006). If an individual perceives an authority figure to be illegitimate, they will feel the authority figure is out of step with their own personal moral values, is untrustworthy, should not be in power, and that they have no obligation to obey that authority (Darling et al., 2005; Darling et al., 2008; de Cremer & Tyler, 2007; Fine et al., 2021; Sunshine & Tyler, 2003). Legal cynicism is related to legitimacy but differs in that it is an attitude about the cultural and societal norms surrounding the law (Hickman et al., 2004; Kirk & Matsuda, 2011; Sampson & Bartush, 1998). Someone with high legal cynicism has little respect for the social norms that support the law and, similar to legitimacy, that cynicism will contribute to an individual's belief that they do not need to obey the law (Kirk & Matsuda, 2011).

Both legal cynicism and perceived legitimacy are impacted by perceptions of procedural justice and, perhaps unsurprisingly, both legal cynicism and perceived legitimacy are associated with a greater degree of antisocial rule-breaking (Kirk & Matsuda, 2011; Trinkner & Cohn, 2014; Tyler & Trinkner, 2017). In short, individuals who perceive authority figures as carrying out procedures in an unfair and unjust manner will also perceive that authority to be illegitimate and will have high legal cynicism. Because they perceive the law as illegitimate, their cynicism towards it will also be high. As a result, this particular individual will disobey the law and break its institutional rules (Trinkner & Cohn, 2014; Tyler & Trinkner, 2017). Conversely, when an individual feels the authority has treated them and others fairly, they will perceive that authority to be legitimate and will have low cynicism towards the social norms surrounding the law and will willingly obey more rules as a result. They feel the law has a claim to make these rules.

Currently, the procedural justice model has only been used to predict antisocial rule-breaking (e.g., Trinkner & Cohn, 2014) and no researcher has yet to determine if it also predicts prosocial rule-breaking. However, because prosocial rule-breaking appears to be driven by a sense that authorities have acted in an unfair manner based on the claims of actual prosocial rule-breakers, the procedural justice model is expected to be a better predictor of prosocial rule-breaking rather than antisocial rule-breaking.

CHAPTER III

GAPS TO ADDRESS

Problems with the Measurement of Moral and Legal Reasoning

What counts as "moral reasoning" or "legal reasoning" remains elusive as there are many competing operational definitions used within the field of psychology. Definitions of moral reasoning range from Kohlberg's classic idea of increasingly developed ability to make reasoned judgements about right and wrong (1971), to the more recent idea of the conscious evaluation of a moral judgment for consistency with moral principles (Paxton & Greene, 2010). Similarly, definitions of legal reasoning range from Tapp and Kohlberg's idea of increasingly developed judgements about laws (1971), to the process of devising, reflecting on, or giving reasons for legal acts (MacCormick, 1998).

Legal socialization researchers have measured moral and legal reasoning in a number of ways, but more recent research has settled on measures of everyday moral reasoning (Cohn et al., 2010; Shelton & McAdams, 1990) and everyday legal reasoning (Cohn et al., 2012) which measure self-reported perceived likelihood to engage in hypothetical behavior across a variety of scenarios about helping and adhering to the law. However, it remains uncertain if responses to these hypothetical scenarios involve reasoning at all as they could just as easily be capturing the more common default moral intuitions and automatic heuristical judgements that do not involve conscious reasoning (Greene et al., 2001). Responses to hypothetical scenarios could be driven by any number of the underlying factors behind moral and legal decision-making and are simply too broad to target the specific concept of reasoning. Furthermore, the use of hypothetical scenarios in self-report questionnaires to measure morality has come under scrutiny due to people acting differently in real moral scenarios than they would report in hypothetical versions of those same scenarios (Feldman-Hall et al., 2012).

One possible solution to these problems is to develop a new scale that targets the specific moral and legal reasons underlying the reasoning process directly rather than assuming self-reported likelihood to engage in behavior is reasoning. The deontological coherence framework offers a way of conceptualizing, understanding, and measuring moral and legal reasoning (Forsyth, 2020; Holyoak & Powell, 2016). This framework arose from the observation that people innately develop and follow internal rules consistent with deontological moral theory as originally proposed by the influential philosopher Immanuel Kant (Greene et al., 2001).

According to Kant, the morally right act is that which conforms to a rule which you wish was a universal law which everyone would follow. This is similar to the Golden Rule (treat others how you wish to be treated) which is found to some degree in virtually every culture and religious system across the globe. While the opposing moral theory "utilitarianism" (do what brings the best consequences) has been shown to be connected with more cognitive processes and offers an alternative normative framework, the deontological "moral law within" (categorical imperative) is more consistent with how people actually think and reason about morality. In short, in his efforts to develop a rationally derived prescriptive normative philosophy, Kant instead outlined a descriptive account of default morality which aligns with people's everyday folk psychology as uncovered by psychological science (Greene, 2008).

While Kant described these internal moral laws as absolute (i.e., moral acts are either permissible or impermissible), modern psychology has identified that different internal rules hold different weights and often conflict. The more valuable a rule is to that individual, the greater the weight. When a person is faced with a moral dilemma, their cognitive process involves shifting the weights of all conflicting rules until they find a coherence that allows for a satisfactory moral judgement (Forsyth, 2020; Holyoak & Powell, 2016). As individuals make more moral judgements over the course of development, the weights of each rule align into a stable coherence pattern that serves as an imprint of prior trends in reasoning.

It is important to note that these internally held deontological rules serve as the *a priori* logical ground that informs moral reasoning when faced with a moral dilemma while simultaneously being adjusted in value if conflicts between rules arise. They are our default judgements that precede and direct our cognitive processes. In short, they are the reasons that guide future reasoning processes. In the case of internal moral rules conflicting with internal rules about legal adherence, the personal value a person attributes to each of these rules should align into a pattern of coherence representing different levels of moral reasoning and legal reasoning.

Because morality is complex with many competing duties and rules, these rules serve more as soft constraints on moral judgements rather than absolute laws that a person will follow in every conceivable circumstance (Holyoak & Powell, 2016). This idea is critical to the modern deontological coherence framework which understands that deontic rules such as "You should always help others" can conflict with other rules such as "You should always follow the law". The rule we choose to follow ultimately depends on individual differences in the personal weight given to each rule when reasoning through past conflicts. These internal deontic rules ultimately serve as the personal reasons that explain our moral decisions (Forsyth, 2020; Holyoak & Powell, 2016), and have generated empirical support that challenges the Kohlbergian view of reasoning.

Because the values of similar rules eventually align into patterns reflective of past reasoning and serve as the guidelines for future moral judgements, all rules related to the moral desire to help others should cluster in an overall measure of moral alignment and rules that are related to the desire to uphold and adhere to the law should cluster into an overall measure of legal alignment. The level of one's moral alignment and legal alignment would be directly representative of past reasoning and predictive of future reasoning processes. A measure of personal value attributed to a series of personally held rules about morality and legality would serve as a direct proxy of moral and legal reasoning while avoiding the pitfalls of scales relying on hypothetical scenarios.

No Existing Measure of Actual Prosocial Rule-Violating Behavior

To differentiate between prosocial rule-breakers and antisocial rule-breakers using the integrated cognitive and the procedural justice models, a measure of prosocial rule-violating behavior is needed. Hennigan and Cohn (2022) previously established that self-reported perceived likelihood to engage in prosocial rule-breaking and antisocial rule-breaking differed across the moral dimensions of prosocial intentions, guilt-proneness, and empathy by having participants respond to hypothetical moral dilemmas. It is possible that the previous hypothetical nature of previous measure of prosocial rule-breaking distorted potential findings in the previous study (Hennigan & Cohn, 2022). A solution to this is to directly ask participants how many times they have broken a series of real-life rules to either help others (prosocial rule-violating behavior) or to help oneself (antisocial rule-violating behavior).

Prior legal socialization research using the Integrated Cognitive Legal Socialization Model and the Procedural Justice Model have used this approach by specifically applying Wolpin's (1983) Delinquency Component of the National Youth Longitudinal Survey. To be consistent with prior legal socialization research, this scale could be adapted into two versions – a prosocial version where each rule-violating behavior is described to specifically help others, and an antisocial version where each rule-violating behavior helps oneself.

Present Studies

While previous research has revealed the existence of prosocial rule-breaking as fundamentally different from antisocial rule-breaking (Hennigan & Cohn, 2022), both constructs must be integrated into existing developmental models before they can have practical benefits. Are prosocial rule-breakers motivated by a sense of injustice or do they simply rationalize self-interested antisocial behavior as moral because it also happens to help others? Do they develop as a result of increased moral reasoning that outweighs their legal reasoning or is prosocial rule-breaking just due to the failure to develop legal reasoning with morality playing no role? For these proposed studies, my goal is to answer these questions by conducting a series of studies that will accomplish the following objectives:

O1. Develop a new measure that distinguishes between morality and legality.

O2. Detect differences in how the Integrated Legal Socialization Model predicts prosocial rule-breaking compared to antisocial rule-breaking.

O3. Detect differences in how the Procedural Justice Legal Socialization Model predicts prosocial rule-breaking compared to antisocial rule-breaking.

O4. Determine what adolescent developmental factors lead to prosocial rule-breaking in adults using the Integrated Legal Socialization Model and the Procedural Justice Legal Socialization Model.

CHAPTER IV

STUDY 1: DEVELOPMENT OF THE LEGAL AND MORAL ALIGNMENT SCALE

The main goal of the proposed study is to expand upon the integrated legal socialization model by developing a self-report measure capable of capturing the two factors of moral reasoning and legal reasoning without relying on only everyday hypothetical scenarios. The proposed scale will be designed to measure the two factors of moral reasoning and legal reasoning across a variety of personally held deontological rules. Using this framework, I have created 28 items with each describing an internally held deontological rule about morality (altruistic prosocial helping) and legality (normative legal adherence) where participants responded on a 7-point Likert scale on how much they agree with the statement described (see appendix A for full item list). Fourteen of these items specifically target alignment to personally held moral principles such as *"You should help others, even if it comes at a personal cost"* and *"It doesn't matter if everyone else is doing it, I won't be immoral to others"*. The remaining 14 items target alignment to the principles of authority and legal adherence such as *"I will always listen to what authority figures tell me"* and *"People who break the law for any reason deserve to get in trouble"*.

The hypotheses are as follows:

1. The items designed to measure moral alignment will load onto a separate subfactor than the items designed to measure legal alignment, but both subfactors will exist under an overall general deontological alignment factor.

2. The moral alignment factor will show convergent validity with morally related constructs such as everyday moral reasoning and discriminant validity with legally related constructs such as everyday legal reasoning.
3. The legal alignment factor will show convergent validity with legally related constructs such as everyday legal reasoning and discriminant validity with morally related constructs such as everyday moral reasoning.

Method

Participants

I recruited 395 college undergraduates through the University of New Hampshire's online subject pool (SONA). I removed 11 individuals who completed the entire study in less than 10 min and 36 who failed to complete the study within the allotted time (2 hours). Of the remaining 348 participants, 277 identified as female (79.8%), 320 primarily identified as White (92.2%), and the average age was 19.1 ($SD = 1.63$). Participants were clustered into specific age group categories during data collection to protect their identity. Each participant received one credit toward course completion for participating.

Materials

Legal and Moral Alignment Scale (LAMAS) Initial Items. The initial 28 items developed for the proposed scale targeted the two factors of moral and legal alignment as described by the deontological coherence framework. The 14 items targeting the moral alignment construct each listed an internal deontological rule about helping others (i.e., the self-held rules used to inform moral reasoning) and the 14 items targeting legal alignment each listed an internally held deontological rule about adherence to the law (i.e., the self-held rules used to inform legal reasoning). Each item asked the participant how likely they would be to break that rule on a scale from 1 (Very Unlikely) to 7 (Very Likely). Because deontological coherence is associated with the universality of internal rules (i.e., these rules are believed to apply to everyone including oneself; Forsyth, 2020; Holyoak & Powell, 2016; Kant, 1785), the items likewise range from rules applying to oneself and to others. For example, one legal item reads: *"If you break the law, you should be punished no matter what"* while another reads: *"I will always follow the law, because that's what I wish everyone did"* Similarly, one moral item reads: *"You should help others, even if it comes at a personal cost"* while another reads *"I will always help others, because that's what I wish everyone did"* Moral Alignment was calculated as the average score of the moral items after eliminating poorly loading items (see the procedure section below) with higher scores indicating greater moral alignment. Legal Alignment was calculated as the average score of the legal items after eliminating poorly loading items with higher scores indicating greater legal alignment.

Everyday Moral Reasoning. To be consistent with prior research using the Integrated Legal Socialization Model (Cohn et al., 2010), I used the 8-item Everyday Moral Reasoning subscale of the Shelton and McAdams' (1990) *Visions of Morality* scale to establish convergent validity with the proposed deontological moral alignment items and discriminant validity with the legal alignment items described above. Each item presents a hypothetical moral behavior and asks participants to rate their likelihood of performing that behavior on a scale ranging from 1 (*I definitely would not do*) to 7 (*I definitely would do*). As an example, one item states: *"The school I attend needs volunteers who will come two hours early one evening next week to help set up for the annual parents' night. I volunteer and come two hours early."* Everyday moral reasoning was calculated as the average of these 8 items after reverse coding relevant items ($M = 4.62$, $SD = 0.81$; $\alpha = .71$), with higher scores reflecting greater everyday moral reasoning.

Everyday Legal Reasoning. Similarly, I used the 16 item Everyday Legal Reasoning Scale (Cole et al., 2013; Cole et al., 2021) to establish convergent validity with legal alignment and discriminant validity with moral alignment. Each item presents a hypothetical moral behavior and asked participants to rate their likelihood of performing that behavior on a 7 point Likert scale ranging from 1 (*I definitely would not do*) to 7 (*I definitely would do*). Example items include: "*I witness a man robbing a store. After the robber is captured, I am asked to talk about what I saw in court. I agree.*" and "*A friend tells me that they have a fake ID to buy alcohol and that they can get me one too. They ask me if I want it. I decline the offer.*" Everyday legal reasoning was calculated as the average of these 7 items with higher scores reflecting greater everyday legal reasoning ($M = 4.18$, $SD = 0.79$; $\alpha = .82$).

Prosocial Intentions. I measured prosocial intentions to help establish convergent validity with the moral alignment factor and discriminant validity with the legal alignment factor using the Prosocial Behavioral Intentions Scale (Baumsteiger & Siegal, 2019). Subjects responded to items on a 7 point Likert scale ranging from *Definitely Would Not Do* to *Definitely Would Do*. Example items include, "*Help a stranger find something they lost, like their key or a pet.*" and "*Help care for a sick friend or relative*". Prosocial intention was calculated as the mean score of these 4 items, with higher scores indicating greater prosocial intentions ($M = 6.08$, $SD = 0.75$; $\alpha = .74$).

Empathy. I measured trait empathy using the Basic Empathy Scale for Adults (BES-A) which was originally developed to measure empathy in young people (Jolliffe & Farrington, 2006) and later adapted to measure empathy in adults (Carré et al., 2013) to help establish convergent validity with the moral alignment factor and discriminant validity with the legal alignment factor. Subjects responded to 20 items on a 5 point Likert scale ranging from *Strongly*

Disagree to *Strongly Agree*. Example items included, "*After being with a friend who is sad about something, I usually feel sad.*" and "*Other people's feelings don't bother me at all.*" (reverse coded). Empathy was calculated as the mean score of these 20 items after reverse-coding relevant items ($M = 3.94$, $SD = 0.46$; $\alpha = .88$), with higher scores indicating higher trait empathy.

Moral Identity. I assessed the two factors of moral identity (internalization and symbolization) using The Self-Importance of Moral Identity Measure (Aquino & Reed, 2002). The internalization sub-factor (internal morality as integral to one's personal identity) was used to help establish convergent validity with the moral alignment factor and discriminant validity with the legal alignment factor. The symbolization sub-factor (symbolic morality as integral to one's public identity) was used to establish nomological validity with the legal alignment factor and convergent validity with the moral alignment factor. The scale begins by listing nine moral characteristics (caring, compassionate, fair, friendly, generous, helpful, hardworking, honest, and kind) and then has subjects respond to 10 items on a 5 point Likert scale (from *Strongly Disagree* to *Strongly Agree*). Example items include, "*It would make me feel good to be a person who has these characteristics*" (internalization) and "*The types of things I do in my spare time (e.g., hobbies) clearly identify me as having these characteristics*" (symbolization). Internalized moral identity was calculated as the mean score of the 5 internalization items after reverse coding relevant items ($M = 3.95$, $SD = 0.44$; $\alpha = .79$), with higher scores indicating a stronger internalized moral identity. Symbolic moral identity was calculated as the mean score of the 5 symbolization items after reverse coding relevant items ($M = 3.95$, $SD = 0.44$; $\alpha = .88$), with higher scores indicating a stronger internalized moral identity.

Obligation to Obey the Law. I measured felt obligation to obey the law using the Rule Orientation Scale (Fine, van Rooij, et al., 2016; Fine & van Rooij, 2021) to help establish convergent validity with the legal reasoning factor and discriminant validity with the moral reasoning factor. Subjects will respond to items on a 7 point Likert scale ranging from *Strongly Disagree* to *Strongly Agree*. Example items include, "*It is acceptable to break a legal rule if this legal rule makes unreasonable demands of you.*" and "*It is acceptable to break a legal rule if you do not understand this legal rule.*" Obligation to obey the law was calculated by reverse coding all 12 items and taking the mean score with higher scores indicating higher felt obligation to obey ($M = 3.85$, $SD = 0.90$; $\alpha = .89$).

Self-Control. I measured self-control using the Brief Self-Control Scale (Tangney et al., 2004) to establish nomological validity with the legal alignment measure and discriminant validity with the moral alignment measure. Subjects responded to items on a 5-point Likert scale ranging from *not at all* to *very much*. Example items include "I am good at resisting temptation" and "I often act without thinking through all the alternatives" (reverse-coded). Self-control was calculated as the mean score of these 13 items after reverse-coding relevant items ($M = 2.81$, $SD = 0.64$; $\alpha = .89$), with higher scores indicating higher self-control.

Prosocial and Antisocial Rule-Breaking Likelihood. Prosocial and antisocial rule-breaking likelihood was measured using the Prosocial and Antisocial Rule-Breaking (PARB) scale (Hennigan & Cohn, 2022) to establish convergent validity with the moral alignment scale (positive for prosocial rule-breaking and negative for antisocial rule-breaking) and the legal alignment scale (negative for both prosocial rule-breaking and antisocial rule-breaking). Prosocial rule-breaking likelihood was measured by taking the average of all prosocial items with higher scores indicating greater prosocial rule-breaking likelihood ($M = 5.04$, $SD = 1.14$, $\alpha = .82$). Antisocial rule-breaking likelihood was measured by taking the average of all antisocial items with higher scores indicating greater antisocial rule-breaking likelihood ($M = 2.32$, $SD = 0.92$, $\alpha = .78$).

Procedure

This study took place entirely online. After being contacted through the University of New Hampshire's SONA system, participants followed a link to a Qualtrics web-based survey. The first page consisted of an informed consent form where participants had to check "agree" before being allowed to continue. Those who checked "disagree" were instead presented with a note thanking them for their time, and they still received class credit without participating. Participants who agreed completed all survey material, including demographic information (gender, age, and race/ethnicity). They were given 2 hours to complete the survey material. This study was approved by the University of New Hampshire's institutional review board (IRB #FY2022-100).

Analytic Strategy

To effectively discern the factor structure underlying the proposed 28 items related to deontological moral and legal reasoning, I utilized an array of analytical methods, starting with the removal of weakly loading items (< .50 on the primary factor) through a principal axis exploratory factor analysis (EFA). Anticipating some cross-loadings between factors, as they are both part of the overall deontological reasoning construct, I opted for an oblimin rotation over an orthogonal rotation (Brown, 2015).

To examine the hypothesized hierarchical structure of the remaining items (moral subfactor and legal subfactor under a general deontological reasoning factor), I adhered to the guidelines proposed by Awang (2012) to compare four SEM models using confirmatory factor analysis – a single factor model, a correlated factors model, a second-order hierarchical model

(Chen et al., 2012; Hull et al., 1991), and a bifactor hierarchical model (Chen & Zhang, 2018; Morin et al., 2016; Reise, 2012). In line with suggestions to avoid correlating residual errors (Brown, 2015; Hermida, 2015; Landis et al., 2009), I adopted a cautious approach and abstained from correlating any error terms to prevent artificially inflating fit statistics. I anticipated that the proposed bifactor model will exhibit the best fit because correlated factors models commonly used in confirmatory factor analyses presume no relation between subfactors (i.e., cross-loadings = 0) and are therefore unsuitable for examining hierarchical models where subfactors are partially accounted for by an overall general factor (Chen et al., 2006). Given the necessity of fixing both paths from the general factor to the two subfactors (Awang, 2012), the second-order model will be equivalent to the correlated factors model and will only serve to provide coefficients for these paths.

The hierarchical bifactor model does not have these limitations, offers fit statistics for the hypothesized hierarchical structure, and enables me to determine the extent to which a construct is explained by the general factor versus subfactors (Giordano & Waller, 2020; Reise et al., 2010). For an in-depth explanation of the advantages of the bifactor model over the second-order model, refer to Chen et al. (2006). Due to the nested nature of these models, I will employ chi-square difference tests to establish if deontological moral reasoning and deontological legal reasoning are best described as unidimensional, two-factor, or a hierarchical construct, with the bifactor model expected to demonstrate a significant improvement over each of the other models tested.

Because Cronbach's α is unsuitable for assessing reliability in multidimensional models (see McDonald, 1999; Rodriguez et al., 2016), I reported McDonald's ω as a reliability coefficient alongside α when evaluating full-scale reliability. The degree of model unidimensionality was reported with omega hierarchical (ωh) with values > .80 indicating a unidimensional model (Rodriguez et al., 2016). Factor loadings for the general factor and two subfactors were derived from the bifactor model by implementing a Schmid Leiman transformation (Ebesutani et al., 2012; Schmid & Leiman, 1957).

Convergent validity with scale measures was established using bivariate correlations. Differences between deontological moral alignment and legal alignment in how they correlate with other scale measures was assessed using Dunn and Clark's z (1969) and Zou's (2007) confidence interval. See Hittner et al. (2003) and Diedenhofen and Musch (2015) for a detailed discussion of why these tests are most appropriate for testing differences between dependent correlations with a shared overlapping variable. I expect the proposed moral reasoning factor to show convergent validity with everyday moral reasoning, prosocial intentions, empathy, guilt-proneness, and moral identity and show discriminant validity with everyday legal reasoning, and obligation to obey the law. I expect the proposed legal reasoning factor to demonstrate the opposite. All SEM model fit statistics will be calculated using AMOS statistical software and all other analyses will be conducted using the *psych* (Revelle, 2019), *jmv* (Selker et al., 2021) and *cocur* (Diedenhofen & Musch 2015) packages in R (R Core Team, 2021).

Hypothesis 1: Identifying Moral and Legal Alignment Subfactors

The EFA on the initial 28 items showed that they generally loaded onto their intended subfactor (Table 1). The Kaiser–Meyer–Olkin measure of sampling adequacy (.883) and Bartlett's test of sphericity ($\chi^2 = 3,327$, $df = 703$, $p < .001$) indicated that the data were suitable for factor analysis. I removed all items with <.50 loading on their main factor, with 10 legal alignment items (α = .90) and eight moral alignment items (α = .81) remaining. The 10 legal

Table 1

Factor Loadings for Initial 28 Items

Item	Factor	
	Legal	Moral
LA1 – I will always follow the law no matter what.	**.81**	
LA2 - If you break the law, you should be punished no matter what.	**.71**	
LA3 - I will always listen to what authority figures tell me.	**.67**	
LA4 - People who break the law for any reason deserve to get in trouble.	**.68**	
LA5 – It's okay to break the law if no one gets hurt.	-.45	
LA6 - I will always follow the law, because that's what I wish everyone did.	**.78**	
LA7 - You should still obey the law, even if the law is not always fair.	**.67**	
LA8 - It's more important to follow the rules than to try and do things your way.	**.60**	
LA9 - I will always try and follow the norms of society.	.43	
LA10 - The world would be a much better place if everyone just did as they were told.	**.62**	
LA11 - You should always obey the law, even if it comes at a personal cost.	**.71**	
LA12 - If you legally hurt others to get ahead, you are not doing anything wrong.		-.33
LA13 - The law is what tells us the difference between right and wrong.	**.61**	
LA14 - It is not necessary to help another person if there is no law saying I have to.		-.44
MA1 - I don't care what other people think, I will always do the morally right thing.		**.50**
MA2 - You should put other people's needs ahead of your own.		.37
MA3 - I always help other people in need, even if its risky.		**.62**
MA4 - You should help others, even if it comes at a personal cost.		**.60**
MA5 - Helping others at a personal cost is for the weak.		-.36
MA6 - I will always help others, because that's what I wish everyone did.		**.65**
MA7 - It doesn't matter if everyone else is doing it, I won't be immoral to others.		**.53**
MA8 - It's more important to be good to people than to go along with the crowd.		.48
MA9 - I will always do what I can to help people, even if most people think its weird.		**.68**
MA10 - You should take the time to help a stranger in need, even if you get nothing out of it.		**.58**
MA11 - I will always help others, no matter what.		**.59**
MA12 - People who legally hurt others to get ahead are not getting the punishment they deserve.		.33
MA13 - If the law never existed, we would still know the difference between right and wrong.		
MA14 - You should always do the morally right thing, even if it's illegal.	-.37	.42
Eigenvalue	5.54	3.64
% Variance Explained	19.72	14.24

Note. 'Principal axis factoring' extraction method was used in combination with an 'oblimin' rotation with a two-factor solution. Loading values > .30 are shown with values > .50 highlighted in bold.

alignment items and eight moral alignment items were combined to create the 18 item Legal and Moral Alignment Scale (LAMAS; α = .84, ω = .85). See Appendix A for the final LAMAS items.

Of all the models tested, the hierarchical bifactor model demonstrated the best fit (comparative fit index [CFI] = .95, Tucker–Lewis index [TLI] = .93, root mean square error of approximation [RMSEA] = .055; χ^2 = 236, df = 117, p < .001; Table 2), with chi-square difference tests showing a large significant improvement over the unidimensional single-factor model (χ^2 = 726, df = 1, p < .001) and a smaller but significant improvement over the correlated-factors model (χ^2 = 87, df = 17, p < .001). Consistent with this, loadings indicated that the hypothesized subset factor structure was retained after controlling for the overall general factor,

Table 2

SEM Model Fit Measures for Study 1 and Study 2

		RMSEA 90% CI				Model Test		
	RMSEA	Lower	Upper	CFI	TLI	χ^2	df	p-value
Study 1 (College Sample)								
Single Factor Model	.13	.13	.14	.64	.59	962	135	< .001
Correlated Factors Model	.06	.06	.07	.92	.91	323	134	< .001
Hierarchical Bifactor Model	**.05**	**.04**	**.06**	**.95**	**.93**	**236**	**117**	**< .001**
Study 2 (MTurk Sample)								
Single Factor Model	.18	.17	.19	.63	.58	1446	135	< .001
Correlated Factors Model	.09	.09	.10	.90	.89	493	134	< .001
Hierarchical Bifactor Model	**.09**	**.08**	**.10**	**.93**	**.90**	**383**	**117**	**< .001**

Note: The fit statistics for the second-order model are identical to the correlated factors model due to both paths to subfactors being fixed and are thus not reported (see Awang, 2012; Chen et al., 2012). Bifactor fit statistics are reported for the hierarchical factors model.

with all items loading more strongly on the subset factors than the general rule-breaking factor (Table 3). As expected, the scale was not unidimensional ($\omega_h = .18$), falling well below the omega-hierarchical threshold of .80 (Rodriguez et al., 2016). This provides support for the existence of moral alignment as a separate construct from legal alignment and indicates that morality and legality are not a single factor.

Table 3

LAMAS Scale General and Subset Factor Loadings for Study 1 and Study 2

	Study 1 (College Sample)			Study 2 (MTurk Sample)		
	General	Legal	Moral	General	Legal	Moral
LA1	.28	.74		.53	.61	
LA2	.23	.69		.45	.64	
LA3	.23	.64		.50	.66	
LA4	.24	.66		.44	.59	
LA6	.30	.73		.54	.62	
LA7	.21	.64		.45	.61	
LA8		.56		.44	.59	
LA10	.20	.59		.40	.63	
LA11	.25	.68		.51	.65	
LA13		.59		.38	.52	
MA1			.49	.41		.42
MA3	.20		.61	.47		.57
MA4			.52	.41		.55
MA6	.25		.64	.46		.66
MA7			.47	.22		.25
MA9	.24		.68	.50		.66
MA10			.51	.42		.64
MA11	.26		.61	.55		.66
Eigenvalues	0.89	4.28	2.62	3.7	3.8	2.6

Note. Loading values > .20 are shown with values > .40 highlighted in bold. Subset factor structure was retained after controlling for the overall general factor with all items loading more strongly on their subset factor than the overall general rule-breaking factor. Displayed values are drawn from each study's respective hierarchical bifactor model using a Schmid Leiman transformation.

Hypothesis 2: Associations with Moral Alignment

Zero-order bivariate correlations demonstrated expected convergent validity with all other constructs with the exception of moral identity (Table 4). As hypothesized, Moral Alignment was positively associated with morally related constructs such as prosocial intentions ($r = .42, p < .001$), empathy ($r = .31, p < .001$), the moral identity internalization factor ($r = .36, p < .001$), the moral identity symbolization factor ($r = .29, p < .001$), prosocial rule-breaking ($r = .20, p < .001$) and was negatively associated with antisocial rule-breaking ($r = -.21, p < .001$). As expected, Moral Alignment showed discriminant validity with obligation to obey the law (i.e., rule orientation; $r = -.04, p = .433$) and self-control ($r = .08, p = .142$).

Hypothesis 3: Associations with Legal Alignment

Legal alignment was not associated with morally related constructs showing no relation to prosocial intentions ($r = .03, p = .604$), empathy ($r = -.04, p = .406$), or the moral identity internalization factor ($r = .09, p = .078$), but was positively associated with the moral identity symbolization factor ($r = .30, p < .001$) possibly hinting to the shared normative concerns of both moral symbolization and legal alignment. However legal alignment was associated with legally related constructs such as obligation to obey the law (i.e., rule orientation; $r = .46, p < .001$), self-control ($r = .24, p < .001$), prosocial rule-breaking ($r = -.41, p < .001$) and antisocial rule-breaking ($r = -.14, p = .009$).

Importantly, correlations with Moral Alignment differed from correlations with legal alignment for prosocial intentions ($r_{difference} = -.45, z = -6.70, p < .001$), empathy ($r_{difference} = -.41, z = -5.94, p < .001$), moral identity internalization ($r_{difference} = -.33, z = -4.78, p < .001$), but not moral identity symbolization ($r_{difference} = .03, z = 0.41, p = .684$), suggesting a difference in the moral motivations underlying moral and legal alignment with the exception of moral identity

Table 4

Correlations Showing Convergent and Discriminant Validity with Legal and Moral Alignment

	Study 1			Study 2		
	Legal Alignment	Moral Alignment	$r_{Difference}$	Legal Alignment	Moral Alignment	$r_{Difference}$
Prosocial Intentions	.03 (0.09%) $p = .604$	**.42** (17.64%) $p < .001$	**-.45** $z = -6.70$ $p < .001$	.08 (0.64%) $p = .168$	**.48** (23.04%) $p < .001$	**-.39** $z = -6.33$ $p < .001$
Empathy	-.04 (0.16%) $p = .406$	**.31** (9.61%) $p < .001$	**-.41** $z = -5.94$ $p < .001$	-.02 (0.09%) $p = .677$	**.37** (13.69%) $p < .001$	**.39** $z = 6.33$ $p < .001$
Moral Identity *Internalization*	.09 (0.01%) $p = .078$	**.36** (12.96%) $p < .001$	**-.33** $z = -4.78$ $p < .001$	.04 (0.16%) $p = .513$	**.37** (13.69%) $p < .001$	**-.35** $z = -5.07$ $p < .001$
Moral Identity *Symbolization*	**.30** (9.00%) $p < .001$	**.29** (8.41%) $p < .001$	.03 $z = 0.41$ $p = .684$	**.34** (11.56%) $p < .001$	**.36** (12.96%) $p < .001$	-.02 $z = -0.37$ $p = .704$
Self-Control	**.24** (5.76%) $p < .001$	.08 (0.64%) $p < .142$	**.17** $z = 2.42$ $p = .015$	**.17** (2.89%) $p < .004$	**.21** (4.41%) $p < .001$	-.04 $z = -0.57$ $p = .569$
Obligation to Obey	**.46** (21.16%) $p < .001$	-.04 (0.02%) $p < .443$	**.51** $z = 7.59$ $p < .001$	**.33** (10.89%) $p < .001$	**.11** (1.21%) $p < .047$	**.22** $z = 3.40$ $p < .001$
Prosocial Rule-Breaking	**-.41** (16.81%) $p < .001$	**.20** (4.00%) $p < .001$	**.64** $z = -9.49$ $p < .001$	**-.31** (9.61%) $p < .001$	-.02 (0.04%) $p = .03$	**-.29** $z = 4.48$ $p < .001$
Antisocial Rule-Breaking	**-.14** (1.96%) $p = .009$	**-.21** (4.41%) $p < .001$	.14 $z = 1.93$ $p = .052$	.08 (0.64%) $p = .190$	**-.12** (1.44%) $p = .041$	**.20** $z = 2.98$ $p = .003$

Note. Significant values are highlighted in bold. Variance explained reported in parentheses. Differences between Legal Alignment and Moral Alignment correlations are calculated using Dunn and Clark's Z procedure.

symbolization. Furthermore, correlations with legal alignment differed from correlations with Moral Alignment across legal dimensions such as those for obligation to obey (i.e., rule orientation; $r_{\text{difference}} = .51$, $z = 7.59$, $p < .001$), self-control ($r_{\text{difference}} = .17$, $z = 2.42$, $p = .015$), prosocial rule-breaking ($r_{\text{difference}} = .64$, $z = -9.49$, $p < .001$) and antisocial rule-breaking ($r_{\text{difference}} = .14$, $z = 1.93$, $p = .052$).

Discussion

The LAMAS Scale demonstrates potential as an instrument for measuring both moral alignment and legal alignment. In general, both alignment subscales exhibited strong convergent and discriminant validity in relation to their theoretically associated constructs, indicating that internal moral motivations differ between moral and legal alignment. Moral alignment seems to be positively associated with prosocial intentions, empathy, and moral identity, while legal alignment does not have an association with these same factors with the exception of moral identity symbolization. This shared association may be due to the normative aspect of legal alignment where the focus is on adherence to social norms and the general social order. Because the symbolization of moral identity is associated with moral appearances rather than internal moral integrity, it makes sense that a normative component is shared with both.

Additionally, legal alignment is associated with legally oriented factors such as obligation to obey the law, and rule-breaking of both types. Self-control has long been associated with rule-following and the findings from Study 1 support this with an association with legal alignment but not with moral alignment. Lastly, and most important to this dissertation, moral alignment is positively associated with prosocial rule-breaking and negatively associated with antisocial rule-breaking as hypothesized. This is consistent with previous theoretical research on prosocial rule-breaking showing that morality and legality associate differently with the two types of rule-breaking (Hennigan & Cohn, 2022).

The LAMAS scale shows the potential for greater nuance when predicting different types of rule-breaking that is currently lacking in current scales measuring moral/normative alignment (Jackson et al., 2012a, 2012b; Sun et al., 2018; Tyler & Jackson, 2018). These existing scales only measure the single factor of belief in shared values between authority and the individuals without measuring what those values actually are (Jackson et al., 2012a). The LAMAS scale distinguishes between the deontological moral principles held by an individual and the legal principles held by the larger social order and enforced by authority.

Intriguingly, the absence of a connection between moral alignment and the moral identity symbolization factor implies that moral alignment is focused on one's internal moral identity rather than one's moral appearance in the context of matching social norms. The association between moral alignment and prosocial rule-breaking implies that prosocial rule-breaking might be driven by internal moral principles and mitigated by the wish to present oneself as moral in public. This is logical, as moral rebels and prosocial rule breakers, like whistleblowers, often face public disapproval (Hennigan, 2015; Minson & Monin, 2012; Touchton et al., 2020). Individuals concerned with preserving public favor should be less inclined to engage in prosocial rule-breaking due to the repercussions that come with violating social norms. On the other hand, those with robust internal moral values who are less preoccupied with their public image should be more prone to engage in prosocial rule-breaking. These results are in line with these notions.

CHAPTER V

STUDY 2: EXPERIMENTAL TEST OF PREDICTIVE DIFFERENCES BETWEEN PROSOCIAL AND ANTISOCIAL RULE-BREAKING

The primary purpose of Study 2 was to expand the integrated legal socialization model with the new moral and legal alignment measures and to determine if the revised model predicts prosocial rule-breaking differently than antisocial rule-breaking. The secondary purpose was to take a confirmatory approach with the LAMAS scale and determine if its factor structure and its relation to theoretically related constructs remained consistent in a different population in comparison to the undergraduate sample of Study 1. There were three main goals of this study. First, I aim to incorporate the newly developed LAMAS scale from Study 1 into the integrated legal socialization model by placing the moral and legal alignment variables just prior to the everyday moral and legal reasoning variables as they theoretically precede the reasoning process (see Study 1). Second, I aim to determine if the integrated model predicts prosocial rule-breaking differently than antisocial rule-breaking. Third, I aim to determine if the procedural justice model predicts prosocial rule-breaking differently than antisocial rule-breaking. The hypotheses were as follows:

1. The factor structure of the LAMAS scale and its relation with other measures would be consistent with Study 1.
2. The integrated model will show a better fit after including the deontological moral and legal alignment variables as covariates in place of everyday moral and legal reasoning scales.

3. The integrated model will show that those with high moral alignment and low legal alignment will engage in prosocial rule-breaking and this will differ from antisocial rule-breaking which will be predicted by low moral alignment and low legal alignment.

Method

Participants

A sample of 301 participants was recruited from Amazon MTurk. This number was chosen based on a power analysis conducted using G*Power statistical software to determine the sample size required to detect an effect size equal to 10% variance explained at the .05 alpha level with .95 power for a multiple regression with 9 planned predictors (see planned analyses below). Results indicated a desired sample size of 110. This number was doubled to account for those in the two conditions and increased to 300 to account for expected loss of data from bots and data cleaning. I removed 10 individuals who completed the entire study in less than 10 min and another 10 for failing to complete the study within the allotted two hours. Of the remaining 281 participants, 145 identified as female (51.6%), 226 primarily identified as White (80.4%), and the average age was 44.5 ($SD = 12.18$). Participants were compensated 3 dollars for completing all survey materials.

Measures

Study 1 Validity Measures. I included all scales used to determine validity from the previous study, including the Prosocial Behavioral Intentions Scale ($M = 5.82$, $SD = 0.94$; $\alpha = .79$); the Basic Empathy Scale in Adults ($M = 3.74$, $SD = 0.62$; $\alpha = .91$); the Self-Importance of Moral Identity Measure ($M = 3.67$, $SD = 0.60$; $\alpha = .76$), with its internalization ($M = 4.23$, $SD = 0.72$; $\alpha = .80$) and symbolization ($M = 3.11$, $SD = 0.97$; $\alpha = .89$) subfactors; the Brief Self-

Control Scale ($M = 3.52$, $SD = 0.82$; $α = .89$); and the Rule Orientation Scale ($M = 4.33$, $SD = 1.25$; $α = .93$), which we used as a measure of felt obligation to obey the law (Fine & van Rooij, 2021).

Legal and Moral Alignment Scale (LAMAS). The final LAMAS scale developed and described in Study 1 was used to measure deontological Moral Alignment ($M = 5.35$, $SD = 1.18$, $α = .81$) and Legal Alignment ($M = 5.35$, $SD = 1.18$, $α = .90$).

Prosocial and Antisocial Rule-Breaking Likelihood. Prosocial and antisocial rule-breaking likelihood will be measured using the Prosocial and Antisocial Rule-Breaking (PARB) scale (Hennigan & Cohn, 2022). Prosocial rule-breaking likelihood will be measured by taking the average of all prosocial items with higher scores indicating greater prosocial rule-breaking likelihood ($M = 5.35$, $SD = 1.18$, $α = .85$). Antisocial rule-breaking likelihood will be measured by taking the average of all antisocial items with higher scores indicating greater antisocial rule-breaking likelihood ($M = 5.35$, $SD = 1.18$, $α = .82$).

Prosocial Rule-Violating Behavior (PRVB). Actual prosocial rule-violating behavior was measured using an adapted version of Wolpin's (1983) Delinquency Component of the National Youth Longitudinal Survey to help establish convergent validity with the moral alignment scale (positive for prosocial rule-breaking and negative for antisocial rule-breaking). This scale was chosen because of its past use in legal socialization research (e.g., Cohn et al., 2010; Trinkner & Cohn, 2014). Participants reported how many times in the last six months they have engaged in 27 rule-violating behaviors. To capture prosocial rule-violating behavior rather than general delinquency, the wording of each item was adapted to specify how many times they broke the rule to help others. Example items include *"hit or seriously threatened to hit someone to help others"*, and *"knowingly stole or held stolen goods to help others"* (see Appendix B for full item list). A variety rule-violating score was created based on recommendations from validity studies (Sweeten, 2012) and to be consistent with prior legal socialization research (see Cohn et al., 2010). Prosocial rule-violating behavior was measured using a count measure by summing the variety of rules broken during the previous 6 months with higher scores indicating greater prosocial rule-violating behavior ($M = 3.53$, $SD = 2.83$). Participants received the PRVB scale when in the Prosocial RVB experimental condition.

Antisocial Rule-Violating Behavior (ARVB). Actual antisocial rule-violating behavior will be measured exactly as prosocial rule-violating behavior except that the wording will be adjusted to replace "*for others*" with "*for yourself*" ($M = 3.53$, $SD = 2.83$; see Appendix B for full list of item wording). Participants received the ARVB scale when in the Antisocial RVB experimental condition.

Everyday Legal Reasoning (ELR). The everyday legal reasoning scale described in study 1 will be used again here (Cole et al., 2013; Cole et al., 2021; $M = 5.35$, $SD = 1.18$, $\alpha = .82$).

Everyday Moral Reasoning (EMR). The everyday moral reasoning scale described in study 1 will also be used again here (Shelton and McAdams, 1990; $M = 5.35$, $SD = 1.18$, $\alpha = .71$).

Normative Status (NS). To measure normative status, I will ask participants "*how much do you approve of...*" the same 27 different rule-violating behaviors drawn from Wolpin's (1983) delinquency measure to create the PRVB and ARVB measures described above. Participants will rate how much they approve of each rule-violating behavior on a scale of 1 (*Strongly Disapprove*) to 4 (*Strongly Approve*). Those in the Prosocial RVB condition will have the added phrase "*for others*" after each item while those in the Antisocial RVB condition will have the added phrase *"for yourself"*. Normative Status will be calculated by taking the average of all 27 items with higher scores indicating greater approval for rule-violating behaviors (see Cohn et al., 2010; M = 5.35, SD = 1.18, α = .94).

Enforcement Status (ES). To measure enforcement status, I will ask participants *"Should people be punished for the following behaviors?"* using the same 27 different rule-violating behaviors described above. Participants will rate how much they believe that each behavior should be punished on a scale from 1 (*No, definitely not*) to 4 (*Yes, definitely*). Those in the Prosocial RVB condition will have the added phrase *"for others"* after each item while those in the Antisocial RVB condition will have the added phrase *"for yourself"*. Enforcement Status will be calculated by taking the average of all 27 items with higher scores indicating greater belief that rule-violating behavior should be punished (see Cohn et al., 2010; M = 5.35, SD = 1.18, α = .94).

Procedure

This study was conducted entirely online. Participants were contacted through Amazon MTurk and given a link to a Qualtrics web-based survey. The first page consisted of an informed consent form where participants had to check agree before being allowed to continue. Those who checked disagree were instead presented with a note thanking them for their time. Participants who agreed were then forwarded to the survey where they were immediately placed into either the Prosocial RVB condition or the Antisocial RVB condition. Those in the Prosocial RVB condition received the prosocial version of the RVB, normative status, and enforcement status scales where the rules being described were followed by *"for others"*. Those in the Antisocial RVB condition received the antisocial version of the RVB, normative status, and enforcement status scales where the rules being described were followed by *"for yourself"*. Participants then completed all survey material including demographic information where they reported their gender, age, racial identity, and ethnicity. Participants will be given two hours to complete the survey material. This study was approved by the University of New Hampshire's Institutional Review Board (IRB #FY2022-186).

Results

Analytic Strategy

Using a confirmatory approach to validate the LAMAS scale, I tested the same SEM models and bivariate correlations from Study 1. To determine the fit of the expanded integrated legal socialization model, I first conducted a generalized structural equation model using a generalized structural equation model (GSEM) to predict prosocial rule-violating behavior and antisocial rule-violating behavior, each of which are count variables of the number of rules violated in the prior 6 month period. Rather than using a typical structural equation model (SEM), I am choosing to use a generalized SEM due to each RVB measure being a negative binomially distributed count variables. The prosocial rule-violating behavior and antisocial rule-violating behavior measures were both expected to conform to a negative binomial distribution where they would be positively skewed and overdispersed. Such distributions are expected among count variables and violate several assumptions of ordinary least squares linear regressions (Warner, 2020), but are appropriately modelled by negative binomial regressions (Dobson & Barnett, 2018; Hilbe, 2011). Unfortunately, standard structural equation models are unable to accommodate negative binomial distributed variables due to SEMs using maximum likelihood estimation which are only compatible with normally distributed continuous variables. While it's true that maximum likelihood estimation *can* estimate the parameters of non-normal distributions in other settings or in a purely mathematical abstract sense, when used in structural equation modelling, it is necessarily set to estimate the parameters of *normal* distributions as this is a necessary assumption for the statistical models indicated in structural equation models and all other statistical models based on normal distributions (i.e., SEM path models are based on correlations which require normality). Thus, generalized structural equation models are required.

While generalized structural equation models do offer some fit indices (Akaike's Information Criterion [AIC], Bayesian Information Criterion [BIC], and proportion of reduction of error [R^2]), they are unable to provide indirect effects. This creates an additional issue for the second hypothesis where I was interested in which paths differ when the model is predicting prosocial rule-breaking versus antisocial rule-breaking (which I will address below). To test for these differences, I conducted a moderated mediation analysis where rule-breaking type (dummy coded as Prosocial=0, Antisocial=1) will moderate all paths to rule-violating behavior. Significant interaction terms will indicate which paths differ between conditions.

Due to the expected negative binomial distribution of the rule-violating behavior variables, I will not be able to calculate indirect effects using Baron and Kenny's product method (1986) but will instead employ a counterfactual approach testing for natural indirect effects. This approach identifies causal pathways by first calculating the total effect (TE) as the difference in the outcome variable between two values of the predictor variable (0 vs 1 for example). It then calculates the natural direct effect (NDE) by taking the change in outcome between the two predictor values after fixing the mediating variable at its expected value as if the predictor was set to 0. Subtracting the NDE from the TE yields the natural indirect effect (NIE; Muthén, et al., 2017; Preacher & Hayes, 2004; Steen, et al., 2017; Valeri & VanderWeele, 2013). The counterfactual framework has been utilized extensively for estimating indirect effects for mixed path type models in other disciplines such as public health (Lange, et al., 2017), and, given the limitations of traditional path analysis techniques, has started to gain traction in legal socialization and other social science research (e.g., Augustyn, 2015; Choy et al., 2017; Cole et al., 2021). This approach has the advantage of being compatible with negative binomial distributed dependent variables while still being algebraically equivalent to Baron and Kenny's product method. I will calculate these indirect effects using the *medflex* package in R (Steen, et al., 2017). I expect that all paths from Legal Alignment will not differ between the prosocial and antisocial conditions, but that all paths from Moral Alignment will. I expect higher Moral Alignment to lead to prosocial rule-breaking while lower Moral Alignment will lead to antisocial rule-breaking.

Hypothesis 1: Consistency of LAMAS with Study 1

All confirmatory factor analyses from the previous study were replicated in Study 2 (see Table 2), with the final hierarchical bifactor model once again demonstrating the best fit, however the fit was not quite as good in Study 1 (CFI = .93, TLI = .90, RMSEA = .086; $\chi^2 = 383$, $df = 117, p < .001$). The factor loadings from the final model were consistent with Study 1 except that the general alignment factor demonstrated somewhat stronger loadings. Despite the increased influence of the general factor, subset factors still loaded strongly on their intended subfactors and were replicated across studies (Table 3). Both the Moral Alignment ($\alpha = .81$) and Legal Alignment ($\alpha = .93$) subscales showed good reliability.

Zero-order bivariate correlations were also generally consistent with Study 1, with Moral Alignment positively associating with prosocial intentions ($r = .48, p < .001$), empathy ($r = .37, p < .001$), and moral identity internalization ($r = .37, p < .001$) and with moral identity symbolization ($r = .36, p < .001$). Unlike Study 1, however, Moral Alignment did associate with obligation to obey ($r = .11, p = .047$) and self-control ($r = .21, p < .001$), albeit weakly.

Furthermore, Moral Alignment did not associate with prosocial rule-breaking ($r = -.02, p = .03$) but was negatively associated with antisocial rule-breaking ($r = -.12, p = .041$).

Contrary to Moral Alignment and also consistent with Study 1, Legal Alignment was not associated with prosocial intentions ($r = .08, p = .168$), empathy ($r = -.02, p = .677$), or moral identity internalization ($r = .04, p = .513$), but did associate with moral identity symbolization ($r = .34, p < .001$). Also consistent with Study 1, Legal Alignment was positively associated with the self-control ($r = .17, p = .004$) and obligation to obey the law ($r = .33, p < .001$). Furthermore, Legal Alignment negatively associated with prosocial rule-breaking ($r = -.31, p < .001$) but was not associated with antisocial rule-breaking ($r = .08, p = .190$). As hypothesized, correlations with Moral Alignment once again differed from correlations with Legal Alignment for prosocial intentions ($r_{difference} = -.39, z = -6.33, p < .001$), empathy ($r_{difference} = .39, z = 6.33, p < .001$), and moral identity internalization ($r_{difference} = -.35, z = -5.07, p < .001$) but did not differ for moral identity symbolization ($r_{difference} = -.02, z = -0.37, p = .704$) or for self-control ($r_{difference} = -.04, z = -0.57, p = .569$). Correlations with moral and Legal Alignment also differed for obligation to obey ($r_{difference} = .22, z = 3.40, p < .001$), prosocial rule-breaking ($r_{difference} = -.29, z = 4.48, p < .001$) and antisocial rule-breaking ($r_{difference} = .20, z = 2.98, p = .003$).

Hypothesis 2: Integrated Legal Socialization Model with Moral and Legal Alignment

Including legal and Moral Alignment in the integrated model showed an overall better fit (AIC = 1052.32, BIC = 1095.10; $R^2 = .56$) than the original integrated model that includes everyday moral and everyday legal reasoning (AIC = 1059.10, BIC = 1101.88; $R^2 = .54$). Legal Alignment and Moral Alignment served as the main covariates predicting RVB as mediated by Normative Status and Enforcement Status. Neither Legal Alignment nor Moral Alignment significantly predicted Normative Status but Legal Alignment did predict Enforcement Status (β

= .24, SE = 0.03, p < .001). For the full model, only Legal Alignment predicted RVB (b = .17, SE = .08, p = .022; IRR = 1.19, 95% CI = 1.03, 1.38). However, against expectations, this association was positive rather than the expected negative relation (b = .17, SE = .08, p = .022; IRR = 1.19, 95% CI = 1.03, 1.38). In short, Legal Alignment unexpectedly predicted a 19% increase in rule violating behavior amount for every one-point increase in Legal Alignment score. Consistent with prior legal socialization research, Normative Status positively predicted RVB (b = 1.31, SE = .14, p < .001; IRR = 3.72, 95% CI = 2.80, 4.99) with each point predicting a 372% increase in RVB.

Also consistent with prior research, Enforcement Status negatively predicted RVB (b = -.47, SE = .08, p = .006; IRR = .63, 95% CI = .44, .88) with each additional point predicting a 37% decrease in RVB (see Table 2). The only indirect path to RVB that was significant was the path from Legal Alignment through Normative Status (IE = .14, SE = .06, p = .01). However, unusual positive predictions when negative relations are expected are not uncommon in the

Table 5

Negative Binomial Regression Predicting RVB from Full Integrated Model

Names	Estimate	SE	exp(B)	95% Exp(B) Confidence Interval		z	p
				Lower	Upper		
(Intercept)	0.320	0.093	1.377	1.147	1.654	3.431	<.001
Legal Alignment	**0.174**	**0.076**	**1.190**	**1.025**	**1.380**	**2.287**	**0.022**
Moral Alignment	0.061	0.099	1.063	0.871	1.296	0.618	0.537
Age	-0.038	0.009	0.963	0.947	0.978	-4.404	<.001
Gender	0.158	0.184	1.171	0.818	1.670	0.856	0.392
Race	0.179	0.224	1.196	0.763	1.854	0.801	0.423
SES	0.052	0.050	1.054	0.947	1.172	1.052	0.293
Normative Status (Approval)	1.313	0.139	3.718	2.800	4.993	9.426	<.001
Enforcement Status (Punish)	-0.468	0.169	0.626	0.437	0.877	-2.764	0.006

integrated model and there have been cases showing a positive relation between moral reasoning and RVB (e.g., Cole et al., 2021).

Hypothesis 3: Integrated Legal Socialization Model Moderated by Rule-Breaking Type

The dichotomized Rule-Breaking Type moderator (Prosocial vs Antisocial) was added to the integrated legal socialization model to examine moderation of the direct and indirect pathways when predicting prosocial rule-violating behavior versus antisocial rule-violating behavior. Once again, including legal and Moral Alignment in the integrated model showed an overall better fit (AIC = 1046.80, BIC = 1103.91; R^2 = .59) than the original integrated model that includes everyday moral and everyday legal reasoning (AIC = 1053.07, BIC = 1110.68; R^2 = .57). Results showed that the path from Moral Alignment to Enforcement Status was moderated by Rule-Breaking Type (b = -.13, SE = .07, p = .045) as was the direct path from Moral Alignment to RVB, as predicted (b = -.625, SE = .20, p = .002; IRR = .54, 95% CI = .35, .80). In short, Moral Alignment predicts prosocial rule-violating behavior differently than antisocial rule-violating with a more positive lean towards prosocial RVB and a more negative lean towards antisocial RVB.

The conditional effects of Rule-Breaking Type revealed a significant indirect effect from Legal Alignment through Normative Status on RVB for antisocial rule-breaking (IE = .23, SE = .08, p = .006; Figure 3) but not for prosocial rule-breaking (IE = .06, SE = .08, p = .443; Figure 4). However, no other pathways were moderated. Interestingly, the problematic positive association between Legal Alignment and RVB was only present when predicting Antisocial Rule-Breaking suggesting a potential issue with the adapted Wolpin's (1983) Delinquency Component scale as Legal Alignment associated in the expected direction with all other measures.

Figure 3

Path Coefficients for Antisocial Rule-Breaking Condition

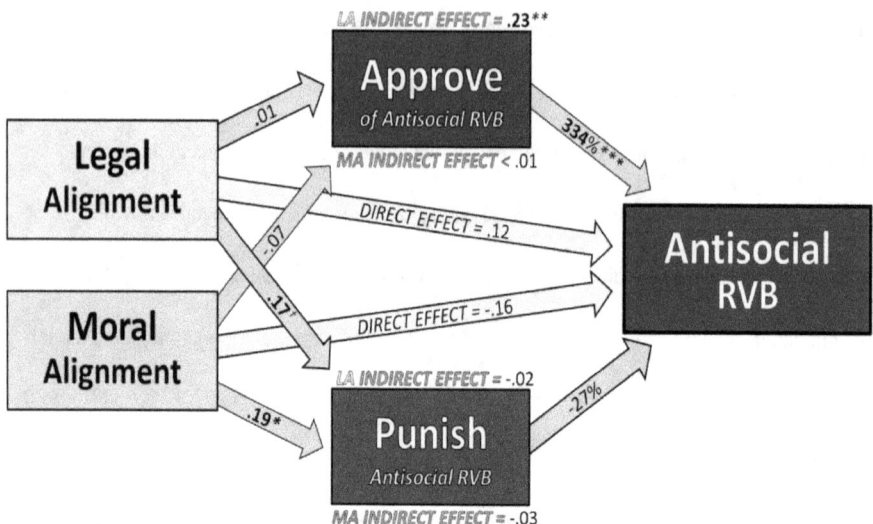

Note: *** $p < .001$, ** $p < .01$, * $p < .05$, † $p < .10$. All values are standardized (β).

Figure 4

Path Coefficients for Prosocial Rule-Breaking Condition

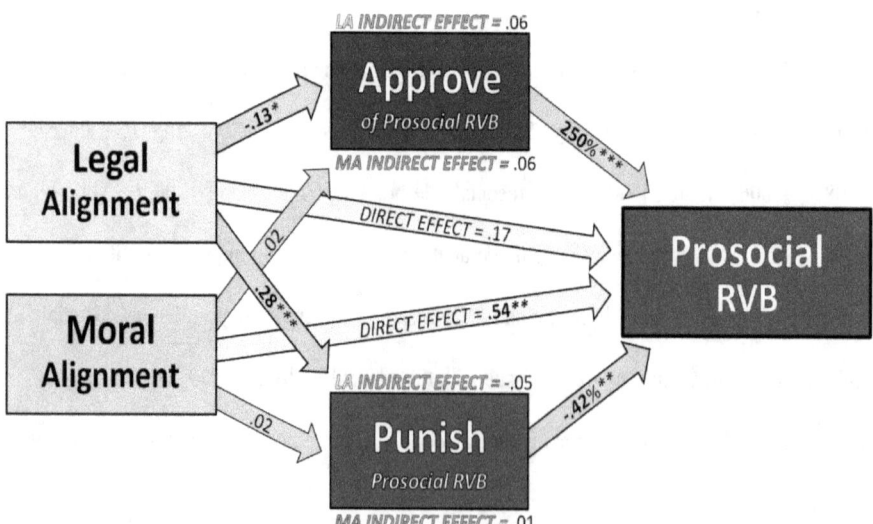

Note: *** $p < .001$, ** $p < .01$, * $p < .05$, † $p < .10$. All values are standardized (β).

Table 6

Negative Binomial Regression Predicting RVB from Moderated Integrated Model

Names	Estimate	SE	exp(B)	z	p
(Intercept)	0.213	0.094	1.237	2.257	0.024
Legal Alignment	**0.182**	**0.074**	**1.200**	**2.466**	**0.014**
Moral Alignment	0.153	0.099	1.165	1.546	0.122
Age	-0.038	0.009	0.962	-4.478	<.001
Gender	0.200	0.179	1.221	1.114	0.265
Race	0.203	0.217	1.225	0.937	0.349
SES	0.033	0.049	1.033	0.678	0.498
RB Type (0 = Pro, 1 = Anti)	**0.591**	**0.186**	**1.806**	**3.182**	**0.001**
Normative Status (Approval)	**1.346**	**0.135**	**3.844**	**9.997**	**<.001**
Enforcement Status (Punish)	**-0.422**	**0.165**	**0.656**	**-2.550**	**0.011**
Legal Alignment ✶ RB Type	-0.166	0.144	0.847	-1.154	0.249
Moral Alignment ✶ RB Type	**-0.625**	**0.197**	**0.535**	**-3.173**	**0.002**
RVB Type ✶ NS (Approval)	0.197	0.256	1.217	0.769	0.442
RVB Type ✶ ES (Punish)	0.266	0.330	1.305	0.806	0.420

Note: Moderated by Rule Breaking Type RB = Rule-Breaking, NS = Normative Status, ES = Enforcement Status

In an exploratory analysis to determine if another measure would better capture the prosocial rule-breaking and antisocial rule-breaking construct, I conducted the analyses again using the Prosocial and Antisocial Rule-Breaking (PARB) Scale (Hennigan & Cohn, 2022) rather than the adapted Wolpin measure (1983). Using traditional SEM models (due to the PARB having normally distributed variables), I conducted two separate analyses for Antisocial Rule-Breaking and Prosocial Rule-Breaking.

The model for Antisocial Rule-Breaking showed poor fit (CFI = .88; RMSEA = .39; χ^2 = 43.8, df = 1, p <.001), likely due to the lack of indirect effects through the mediators (Figure 5). However, the direct effects showed the same unexpected positive association between Legal

Alignment and Antisocial Rule-Breaking ($DE = .11$, $p = .008$) but did have the expected negative association between Moral Alignment and Antisocial Rule-Breaking ($DE = -.09$, $p = .041$).

The model for Prosocial Rule-Breaking also showed a poor fit (CFI = .79; RMSEA = .41; $\chi^2 = 48$, $df = 1$, $p < .001$), similarly due to the lack of indirect effects through the mediators (Figure 6). However, the direct effects showed the expected negative association between Legal Alignment and Prosocial Rule-Breaking ($DE = -.33$, $p < .001$) and the expected positive association between Moral Alignment and Antisocial Rule-Breaking ($DE = -.33$, $p = .009$). Overall, the PARB scale seemed to better model Prosocial and Antisocial Rule-Breaking compared to the adapted Wolpin's (1983) Delinquency Component scale.

Figure 5

Path Coefficients for Antisocial Rule-Breaking Using the PARB Scale

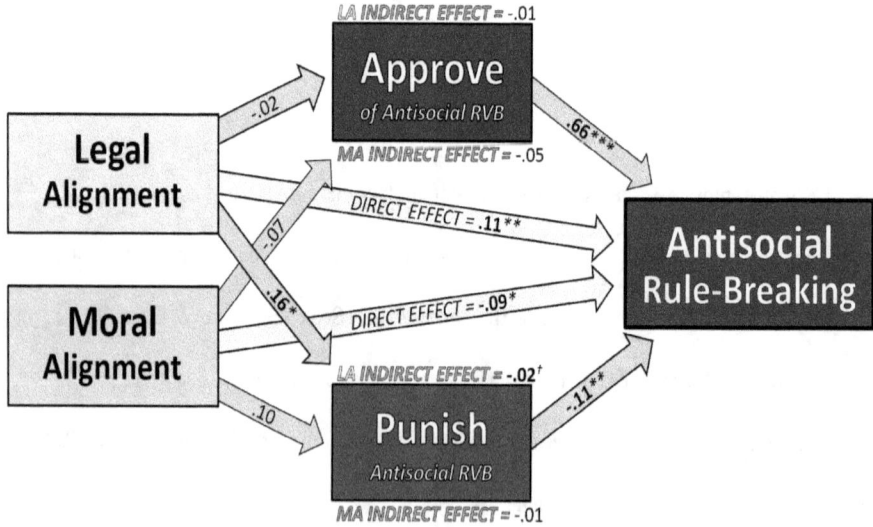

Note: *** $p < .001$, ** $p < .01$, * $p < .05$, † $p < .10$. All values are standardized (β).

Figure 6

Path Coefficients for Prosocial Rule-Breaking Using the PARB Scale

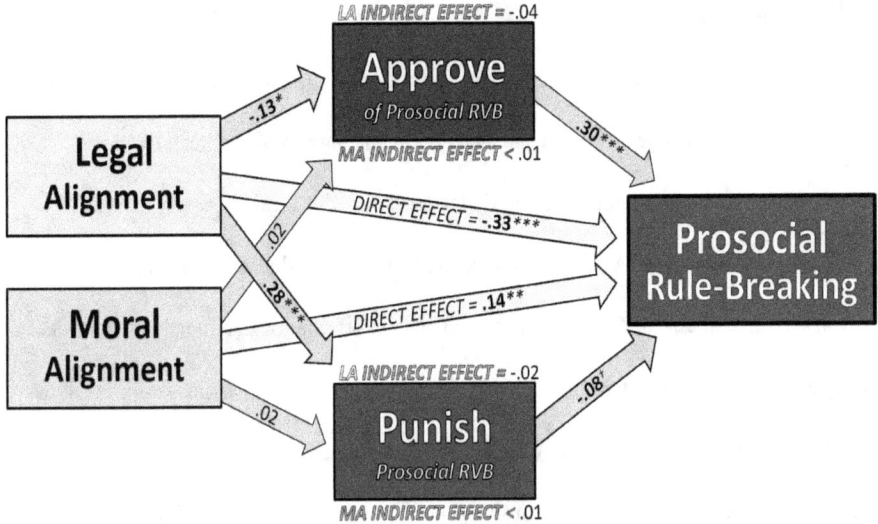

Note: *** $p < .001$, ** $p < .01$, * $p < .05$, † $p < .10$. All values are standardized (β).

Discussion

Study 2 offers additional support for the validity of the LAMAS Scale as a measurement tool that effectively captures the same construct as actual prosocial and antisocial rule-breaking behavior, albeit with certain limitations. Firstly, the hierarchical factor structure of the LAMAS scale identified in Study 1 and the connections between each subscale and relevant theoretical survey measures were generally consistent in both studies. However, the confirmatory factor analysis model fit statistics for the LAMAS factor structure were not quite as good as in Study 1.

As hypothesized, the Integrated Cognitive Legal Socialization model showed a better fit when using the moral alignment and legal alignment scores from the LAMAS than it did when using the original everyday moral reasoning and everyday legal reasoning measures. Consistent with hypotheses, moral alignment predicted prosocial rule-breaking differently from antisocial rule-breaking when used in the Integrated Cognitive Legal Socialization Model. In short, moral alignment predicted prosocial rule-breaking positively while it had a negative trend towards antisocial rule-breaking.

Also as hypothesized, legal alignment scores from the LAMAS scale did not predict prosocial rule-violating behavior and antisocial rule-violating behavior differently in the Integrated Cognitive Legal Socialization Model. Unexpectedly, legal alignment *positively* predicted rule-violating behavior when predicting antisocial rule-breaking which is the opposite of what was hypothesized. This was true for the indirect effect through normative status when using the adapted version of Wolpin's (1983) Delinquency Component scale and for the direct effect when using the Prosocial and Antisocial Rule-Breaking (PARB) Scale. However, this would not be the first study to have also shown similar unexpected reversed directional association when using the integrated model with a recent study showing a positive relation between everyday moral reasoning and RVB (Cole et al., 2021).

There are several reasons as to why this may be the case in the present study. One possibility is that the effect may be distorted by suppression effects as many variables in the integrated model predict RVB in opposite directions which can distort the direction of relationships in unexpected directions (Friedman & Wall, 2005; Paulhus et al., 2004). The second explanation is that moral alignment, approval of rule-violation, and the desire to punish rule-breaking explain more of the variance in antisocial rule-breaking that would otherwise be explained by legal alignment. Approval and desire to punish may be integral to the concept of legal alignment and once you strip these components away, there may be an antisocial component remaining in legal alignment after controlling for moral alignment. In other words, it may be this remaining antisocial component that is positively associating with antisocial rule-breaking after removing the variance shared with moral alignment, belief in punishment, and approval of RVB. This hidden antisocial component could be behind a selfish desire to follow the law solely for the sake of self-preservation rather than a desire for social order or a belief in the greater good that comes with following the law. Once you subtract moral alignment, belief in punishment, and disapproval of rule-breaking from legal alignment, it seems you are left with antisociality that positively associates with antisocial rule-breaking.

Another issue raised by the results of this study is if Wolpin's (1983) Delinquency Component scale can be successfully adapted to measure antisocial and prosocial rule-breaking as well as the previously validated Prosocial and Antisocial Rule-Breaking (PARB) scale (Hennigan & Cohn, 2022). Due to using different analysis techniques to accommodate their different distributions, it is difficult to compare fit statistics when using the integrated model to predict both scales. However, path coefficients suggest the PARB and the adapted Wolpin's scale are both useful measures that similarly predict prosocial and antisocial rule-breaking with some slight differences in indirect and direct pathways.

There are pros and cons to each with Wolpin's scale having an advantage in measuring actual behavior but being at a disadvantage due to different participants having more or less opportunities to engage in such rare behavior in a 6 month period which could confound results. It is not often we are presented with the opportunity to hit or kick someone to help another person for example. Maybe one participant who is extraordinarily prosocial never encountered a situation where someone needed to be physically defended by an attacker, while another unlucky participant encountered numerous situations. Also, it may be confusing for some participants when asked how many times they have broken a law such as hitting or stealing for others or for oneself. They may have difficulty linking the description to real life experiences. Furthermore, the sheer length of the scale may make implementing it impractical. Asking participants to remember the exact amount of times they engaged in each behavior for such a lengthy scale may be mentally taxing.

Unlike the Wolpin's measure, the PARB scale employs self-reported likelihood of engaging in a variety of hypothetical behaviors. The PARB scale is at a disadvantage in that it does not measure behavior directly, but measures a propensity to engage in prosocial and antisocial rule-breaking. However, the advantage is that it controls for the differing opportunities participants may have to engage in prosocial rule-breaking. The PARB scale has also demonstrated great utility in predicting a variety of actual real life prosocial rule-breaking behaviors such as cheating to help others and certain protest behaviors (Hennigan & Cohn, 2022). While both scales are useful and can be used interchangeably in many contexts, further studies should consider these pros and cons when choosing to use the PARB scale over the adapted Wolpin Delinquency Component measure.

CHAPTER VI

STUDY 3: LONGITUDINAL DEVELOPMENT OF PROSOCIAL RULE-BREAKING

This study had two main goals. The first goal of Study 3 was to replicate the integrated model's ability to predict prosocial rule-breaking as demonstrated in Study 2 in a longitudinal study of adolescents who have since grown into adults. The secondary purpose of Study 3 was to determine if the procedural justice legal socialization model predicts prosocial rule-breaking differently than antisocial rule-breaking in the same longitudinal sample. This study used new and existing data from the New Hampshire Youth Study (NSF grant # 1733595). The hypotheses are as follows:

1. The integrated model will show good fit when predicting prosocial rule-breaking over a period of longitudinal development from adolescence to adulthood.
2. The integrated model will show that those with high moral reasoning and low legal reasoning will engage in prosocial rule-breaking and this will differ from antisocial rule-breaking which will be predicted by low moral reasoning and low legal reasoning.
3. The procedural justice model will show good fit when predicting prosocial and antisocial rule-breaking over a period of longitudinal development from late adolescence to adulthood.
4. Perceived unfairness of the police will lead to less legitimacy and greater prosocial rule-breaking and this indirect effect will be greater than the same indirect effect for antisocial rule-breaking.

Method

Participants

Participants were 297 adults who have been long term participants in the New Hampshire Youth Study from about the age of 12 years old. Of these participants, 193 identified as female (65%) and 202 primarily identified as White (68%). The average age of participants was 17.68 ($SD = 1.53$) at Time 1, 18.98 ($SD = 2.09$) at Time 2, and 27.12 ($SD = 3.11$) at Time 3. The number of participants was purely based on the number of respondents to our contact attempts. Participants were contacted in two primary ways. The first was using updated emails that the participants themselves provided to us in the previous waves across all phases of the study. The second was through emails obtained through the software BeenVerified which we have used to track down lost or missing participants. Participants were compensated with a $20 Amazon gift card at Wave 8 (Time 1) and Wave 9 (Time 2) and received a $30 Amazon gift card at Wave 12 (Time 3) for their participation.

Measures

Prosocial and Antisocial Rule-Breaking. Prosocial and antisocial rule-breaking likelihood was measured at Time 3 using the Prosocial and Antisocial Rule-Breaking (PARB) scale (Hennigan & Cohn, 2022). Prosocial rule-breaking likelihood was measured by taking the average of all prosocial items with higher scores indicating greater prosocial rule-breaking likelihood ($M = 4.50$, $SD = 1.32$, $\alpha = .82$). Antisocial rule-breaking likelihood was measured by taking the average of all antisocial items with higher scores indicating greater antisocial rule-breaking likelihood ($M = 1.80$, $SD = 0.98$, $\alpha = .82$).

Everyday Legal Reasoning. The same 16-item Everyday Legal Reasoning scale used in the previous two studies was measured at Time 1 (Cole et al., 2013; Cole et al., 2021). Everyday Legal Reasoning was calculated as the average of these 16 items with higher scores indicating higher legal reasoning ($M = 4.59$, $SD = 1.09$, $α = .95$).

Everyday Moral Reasoning. The 8-item Everyday Moral Reasoning scale used in the previous two studies was measured at Time 1 (Shelton and McAdams, 1990). Everyday Moral Reasoning was calculated as the average of these 8 items after reverse coding relevant items ($M = 4.45$, $SD = 1.16$, $α = .82$), with higher scores reflecting greater everyday moral reasoning.

Normative Status. Normative status was measured at Time 2 where participants were asked, *"how much do you approve of..."* the 27 different rule-violating behaviors drawn from Wolpin's original (1983) delinquency measure. Participants rated how much they approve of each rule-violating behavior on a scale of 1 (*Strongly Disapprove*) to 4 (*Strongly Approve*). Normative Status was calculated by taking the average of all 27 items with higher scores indicating greater approval for rule-violating behaviors (see Cohn et al., 2010; $M = 0.38$, $SD = 0.29$; $α = .92$).

Enforcement Status. Enforcement status was measured at Time 2 where participants rated the degree rule-violating behavior should be punished after being asked, *"Should people be punished for..."* using the same 27 different rule-violating behaviors described above. Participants rated how much they believe that each behavior should be punished on a scale from 1 (*No, definitely not*) to 4 (*Yes, definitely*). Enforcement Status was calculated by taking the average of all 27 items with higher scores indicating greater belief that rule-violating behavior should be punished (see Cohn et al., 2010; $M = 2.26$, $SD = 0.45$; $α = .94$).

Procedural Justice. To measure perceptions of whether police are fair and just in their procedures, participants responded 10 items at Time 1 that were originally drawn from Folger and Konovsky's (1989) and Moorman's (1991) procedural fairness scales and later adapted for use in legal socialization research by Trinkner and Cohn (2014). Example items include: *"The police in your area give you a chance to express your side when you discuss things with them"* and *"The police show concern for your rights as a member of the community"*. Participants responded to each item on a 5-point Likert scale from 1 (*Strongly Disagree*) to 5 (*Strongly Agree*). Procedural justice was calculated by taking the average of the 10 items with higher scores indicating greater belief that the police are procedurally fair ($M = 3.47$, $SD = 0.86$, $\alpha = .97$).

Legitimacy. To measure belief in whether the police are a legitimate authority, participants responded to 10 items that were originally drawn from Sunshine and Tyler's (2003) measure of police legitimacy and later adapted for use in legal socialization research by Trinkner and Cohn (2014). Example items include: *"I agree with many of the values that define what the police stand for"* and *"There are things about the police and their policies that need to be changed"* (reverse coded). Participants responded to each item on a 5-point Likert scale from 1 (*Strongly Disagree*) to 5 (*Strongly Agree*). Procedural justice was calculated by taking the average of the 10 items after reverse coding relevant items with higher scores indicating greater belief that the police are legitimate authority figures ($M = 3.17$, $SD = 0.48$; $\alpha = .84$).

Legal Cynicism. To measure cynicism towards the legal system, participants responded to the 5 items from Trinkner and Cohn's legal cynicism scale (2014). Example items include: *"Rules were meant to be broken"* and *"To make money, there are no right and wrong ways anymore, only easy and hard ways"* Participants indicated their agreement to these five items on a scale of 1 (*Strongly Disagree*) to 5 (*Strongly Agree*). Legal cynicism was calculated as the average of these five items with higher scores indicating greater cynicism towards the legal system ($M = 2.50$, $SD = 0.75$; $α = .74$).

Procedure

Beginning in 2011, the variables used in this study were collected from wave 8 (Time 1), wave 9 (Time 2), and wave 12 (Time 3) of the NHYS. Participants were originally selected from five high schools and seven middle schools in various communities across New Hampshire at the outset of the NHYS. Parental assent was obtained for each participant before being allowed to participate in their first wave. The study originally involved sixth and ninth graders who completed paper surveys roughly every six months (typically in fall and spring) during large group sessions at their respective schools for the initial six waves. When students graduated high school, they were transitioned to an online survey using Qualtrics which was used for all remaining waves. Participants continued to complete online surveys regularly until wave 12 (Time 3).

Wave 12 of the NHYS was similarly conducted online using Qualtrics. Participants were contacted through email and given a link to the Qualtrics based web survey along with a unique study ID number. The first page consisted of a field to enter their study ID number which was later used to connect their responses from prior waves to the current dataset. Participants then completed an informed consent form and were required to check agree before being allowed to continue. Those who check disagree were instead presented with a note thanking them for their time. Participants who agreed were then forwarded to the survey where they completed all survey material. This material also included demographic information where they reported their gender, age, racial identity, and ethnicity. Completing the survey typically took around 20-30 minutes, and upon completion, participants were directed to a separate and disconnected Qualtrics survey to provide their contact information for future communication and to provide contact information to receive their gift cards. This study was approved by the University of New Hampshire's Institutional Review Board and is supported by the National Science Foundation (NSF grant # 1733595).

Analytic Strategy

The same analytic strategy used in Study 2 to examine the integrated model was used here but instead relied on traditional SEM techniques instead of GSEM due to the PARB scale producing normally distributed variables. The same strategy will be used to examine the Procedural Justice Model when predicting both prosocial rule-breaking and antisocial rule-breaking. The only difference will be that the moral alignment and legal alignment measures will be replaced with the original everyday moral reasoning and everyday legal reasoning measures in the Integrated Cognitive Legal Socialization Model due to not existing during time 1 of data collection. However, the expected paths from everyday moral and legal reasoning are expected to replicate similarly as to those from moral and legal alignment. All SEM analyses will include age, race (1 = White), gender (1 = male), and socioeconomic status as control variables.

Results

Bivariate correlations can be found in Table 8. Results show that the integrated model had similar fit to Study 2 when predicting prosocial rule-breaking (CFI = .771, RMSEA = .52; χ^2 = 39.77, df = 1, p < .001) but a slightly worse fit compared to Study 2 when predicting antisocial rule-breaking (CFI = .772, RMSEA = .52; χ^2 = 39.77, df = 1, p < .001). Remarkably, both models had nearly identical fit when predicting prosocial and antisocial rule-breaking. In the integrated model predicting prosocial rule-breaking, the indirect effect from Legal Reasoning and through

Table 8

Study 3 Correlation Matrix

	1.	2.	3.	4.	5.	6.	7.	8.	9.
1. Moral Reasoning	—								
2. Legal Reasoning	.54 ***	—							
3. Approve (NS)	-.28 ***	-.44 ***	—						
4. Punish (ES)	.32 ***	.46 ***	-.46 ***	—					
5. Prosocial Rule-Breaking	.01	-.34 ***	.28 ***	-.35 ***	—				
6. Antisocial Rule-Breaking	-.18 *	-.32 ***	.22 **	-.28 ***	.39 ***	—			
7. Procedural Justice	.25 ***	.40 ***	-.26 ***	.21 ***	-.13	-.10	—		
8. Legitimacy	.15 **	.29 ***	-.28 ***	.32 ***	-.07	-.12	.38 ***	—	
9. Legal Cynicism	-.08	-.19 ***	.30 ***	-.17 ***	.28 ***	.14	-.23 ***	-.26 ***	—

Note. $*p < .05, **p < .01, ***p < .001$

Enforcement Status (punish) was nearly significant ($IE = -.11, SE = .07, p = .074$) but no other indirect paths were (Figure 7). Similar to Study 2, the direct effects show that Legal Reasoning negatively predicted prosocial rule-breaking ($DE = -.32, SE = .14, p < .001$) while Moral Reasoning positively predicted prosocial rule-breaking ($DE = .30, SE = .11, p < .001$). Furthermore, results show that for the integrated model predicting antisocial rule-breaking, the indirect effect from legal reasoning and through Enforcement Status (punish) was significant ($IE = -.16, SE = .04, p = .008$), showing consistency with Study 2. As one's legal reasoning increases, so does the belief that rule-breaking should be punished ($\beta = .60, SE = .03, p < .001$), which in turn leads to less antisocial rule-breaking ($\beta = -.27, SE = .18, p = .005$). However, unlike Study 2, the direct paths were not significant (Figure 8).

The procedural justice model showed good fit when predicting prosocial rule-breaking (CFI = .922, RMSEA = .19; $\chi^2 = 6.20, df = 1, p = .013$), as it did when predicting antisocial rule-

Figure 7

Integrated Model Predicting Prosocial Rule-Breaking in Longitudinal Study

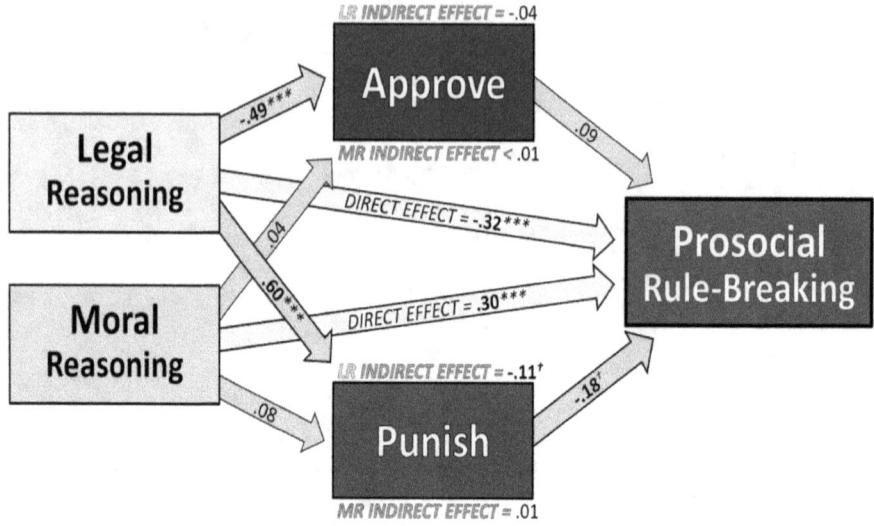

Note: *** $p < .001$, ** $p < .01$, * $p < .05$, † $p < .10$. All values are standardized (β).

Figure 8

Integrated Model Predicting Antisocial Rule-Breaking in Longitudinal Study

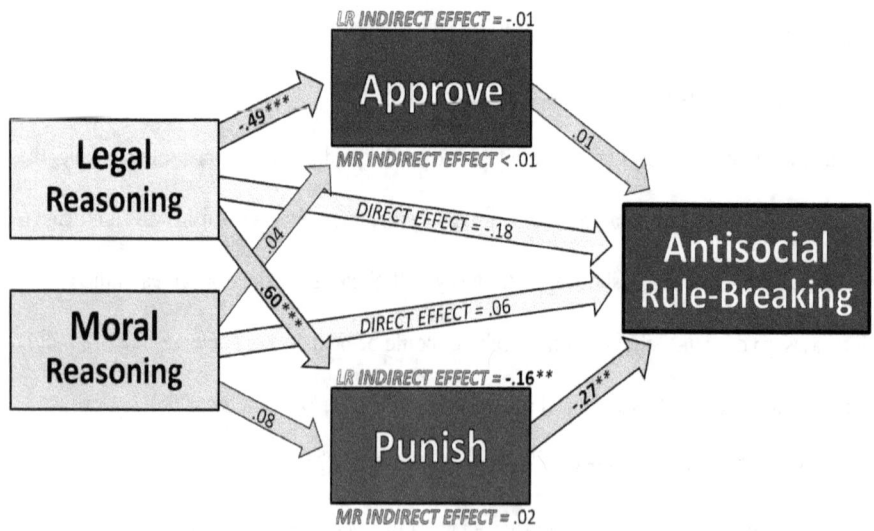

Note: *** $p < .001$, ** $p < .01$, * $p < .05$, † $p < .10$. All values are standardized (β).

breaking (CFI = .915, RMSEA = .19; χ^2 = 6.20, df = 1, p = .013). In the procedural justice model predicting prosocial rule-breaking, the indirect effect through legitimacy was significant (IE = -.10, SE = .06, p = .013) while the path through legal cynicism was nearly significant (IE = .03, SE = .02, p = .050) showing support for a path through legitimacy and potential support for a path through legal cynicism (Figure 9). As perception of police fairness increases, belief in police as a legitimate authority also increases (β = .61, SE = .02, p < .001), which leads to a reduction in prosocial rule-breaking likelihood (β = -.17, SE = .11, p = .012). In the model predicting antisocial rule-breaking, a similar pattern was detected with the indirect path through legal cynicism being almost significant (IE = -.05, SE = .03, p = .076) but with no other significant paths detected.

Figure 9

Procedural Justice Model Predicting Prosocial Rule-Breaking

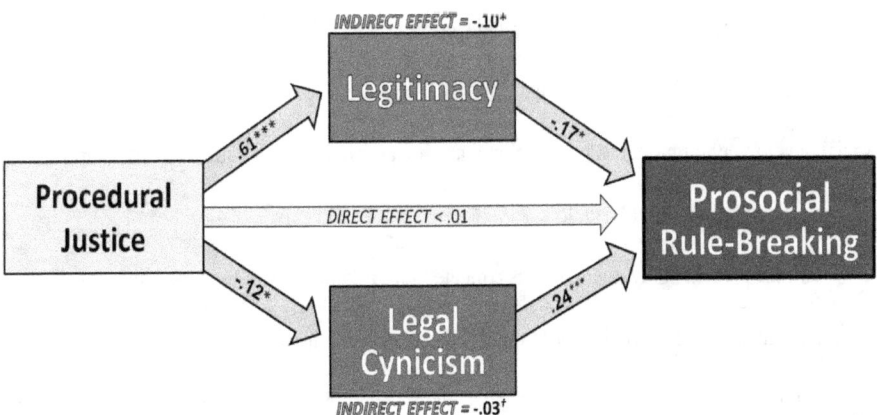

Note: *** p < .001, ** p < .01, * p < .05, † p < .10. All values are standardized (β).

Figure 10

Procedural Justice Model Predicting Antisocial Rule-Breaking

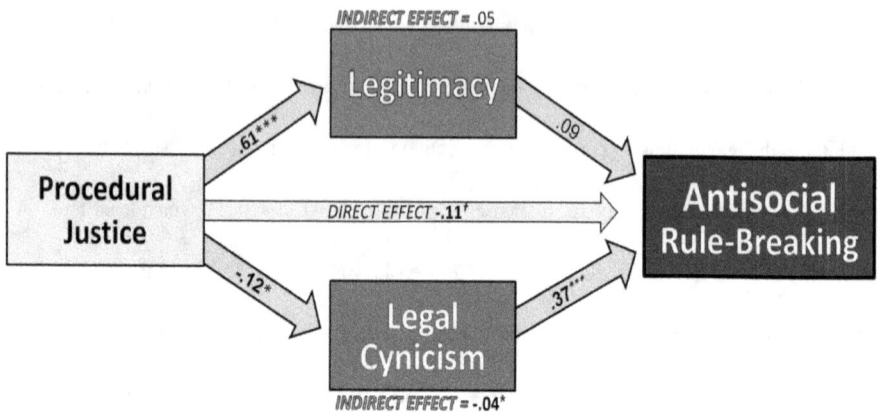

Note: *** $p < .001$, ** $p < .01$, * $p < .05$, † $p < .10$. All values are standardized (β).

Discussion

Study 3 shows some support for a developmental model of prosocial rule-breaking and antisocial rule-breaking using the Integrated Cognitive Legal Socialization Model but with some inconsistencies with the cross-sectional Study 2. The present study also shows support for a social developmental model of prosocial and antisocial rule-breaking using the Procedural Justice Legal Socialization Model.

In the present study, the data was collected longitudinally with the procedural justice and legitimacy measures collected prior to the BLM protests and the prosocial and antisocial rule-breaking measures collected afterwards. This historic event likely had an overall public effect on the perceptions of procedural justice and police legitimacy since the time these variables were measured during the earlier waves of the NHYS. While this event likely had an effect on participants' prosocial rule-breaking likelihood, the social development of this effect through perceptions of police fairness on belief in police as a legitimate authority would not have been captured in the presently available data. Future studies should aim to detect whether this event impacted the mediating variables leading to prosocial and antisocial rule-breaking in a way similar to what we see in the cross-sectional analyses of Study 2 and Study 3, both which took place after the BLM protests.

CHAPTER VII

GENERAL DISCUSSION

The primary purpose of this dissertation was to determine what internal cognitive and external social factors contribute to the development of prosocial rule-breaking as compared to antisocial rule-breaking. Traditionally, researchers across a variety of academic disciplines have narrowly defined rule-breaking as solely antisocial behavior. This definition, however, cannot account for instances of rule-breaking driven by the desire to help others. My research, as described throughout this dissertation, has been an attempt to show that morality is not a single construct, but falls into the two dimensions of a prosocial morality and rule-following legality. These two constructs were then included into the established Integrated Cognitive Legal Socialization Model (Cohn et al., 2010; Cohn et al., 2012) to determine a possible cognitive developmental pathway to the phenomenon of prosocial rule-breaking as opposed to antisocial rule-breaking. Furthermore, I then investigated social developmental pathways using the Procedural Justice Legal Socialization Model (Fagan & Tyler, 2005; Fagan & Piquero, 2007; Piquero et al., 2005; Trinkner & Cohn, 2014; Tyler & Trinkner, 2017) to determine the development of prosocial rule-breaking as opposed to antisocial rule-breaking.

Over the course of these three studies, I have developed and validated the Legal and Moral Alignment Scale (LAMAS) which is capable of distinguishing between morality and legality, used these subfactors as predictors in the integrated model to successfully predict rule-breaking, and used the procedural justice model to determine the social influences that give rise to prosocial rule-breaking in both cross-sectional and longitudinal contexts. This research, I hope, will help dispel the long-held belief that all rule-breakers are inherently antisocial.

Key Findings

In the first study, I developed the LAMAS to measure the two separate concepts of moral alignment and legal alignment. Of the initial 28 items, 13 loaded onto the legal alignment factor which targeted adherence to legal rules and social order, and 8 loaded onto the moral alignment factor with targeted general prosociality and selfless concern for others. As predicted, the moral alignment factor showed convergent and nomological validity with everyday moral reasoning (Shelton & McAdams,1990), prosocial intentions (Baumsteiger & Siegal, 2019), empathy (Carré et al., 2013), internal moral identity, and symbolic moral identity (Aquino & Reed, 2002). Moral alignment also showed discriminant validity with everyday legal reasoning (Cole et al., 2013; Cole et al., 2021), obligation to obey the law (Fine, van Rooij, et al., 2016), and self-control (Tangney et al., 2004). Conversely, legal alignment showed convergent and nomological validity with everyday legal reasoning, obligation to obey the law, symbolic moral identity, and self-control while showing discriminant validity with everyday moral reasoning, prosocial intentions, empathy, and internal moral identity. Moral alignment was positively associated with prosocial rule-breaking and negatively associated with antisocial rule-breaking while legal alignment was negatively associated with both types of rule-breaking. Overall, the first study established the LAMAS scale as a potential measure for disentangling prosociality from rule-breaking.

In the second study, I further validated this scale by replicating the previous findings in a different population and examined the predictive power of moral alignment and legal alignment when included in the Integrated Cognitive Legal Socialization Model (Cohn et al., 2010; Cohn et al., 2012). The second study also utilized a cross-sectional experimental design to investigate the cognitive developmental differences between prosocial and antisocial rule-violating behavior using the integrated model. The findings revealed that when used in the integrated model, moral alignment predicted rule-violating behavior differently depending on if it was prosocial RVB or antisocial RVB with moral alignment only being positively associated with prosocial RVB. The only direct effect was moral alignment positively predicting prosocial RVB and the only indirect effect was a positive relationship from legal alignment to antisocial RVB as mediated by normative status (approval of RVB). However, when using the Prosocial and Antisocial Rule-Breaking (PARB) scale to measure prosocial and antisocial rule-breaking likelihood (Hennigan & Cohn, 2022) both moral and legal alignment had direct effects where moral alignment positively predicted prosocial rule-breaking and legal alignment negatively predicted prosocial rule-breaking. In essence, individuals' moral considerations and understanding of legal principles were found to directly impact their self-perceived propensity to engage in prosocial rule-breaking. However, the anticipated mediating role of attitudes towards rule-breaking was not supported by the findings. In contrast to studies investigating general rule-violating behavior, attitudes towards rule-breaking generally did not mediate the effects of moral or legal reasoning on prosocial rule-breaking. This suggests a more direct relationship between these cognitive processes and rule-breaking behavior that requires further exploration.

In the third and final study, I explored the development of prosocial rule-breaking across three waves of a longitudinal study, employing both the integrated cognitive and procedural justice models. The results indicated that the integrated model could predict prosocial rule-breaking through direct effects from both moral and legal reasoning in the same direction as the moral and legal alignment direct effects from Study 2. However, with the exception of an indirect through enforcement status (belief RVB should be punished) from legal reasoning to rule-breaking, these effects were not found to be mediated by attitudes towards rule-breaking, showing general consistency with Study 2. The results from Study 3 also suggested that the procedural justice model predicted prosocial rule-breaking through an indirect effect from perceived police fairness through legitimacy. In short, the more unfair the police are perceived to treat people, the less legitimate they are believed to be, and the more likely someone will be willing to engage in prosocial rule-breaking.

Implications

The present studies contribute to a growing body of legal socialization research by adapting both legal socialization models and using them to distinguish between prosocial rule-breaking and antisocial rule-breaking. Prosocial rule-breaking is defined here as acts of disobedience performed with the intention of benefiting others or the society at large (Hennigan & Cohn, 2022). Using the Integrated Cognitive Legal Socialization Model and the Procedural Justice Model uncovers developmental differences between prosocial rule-breaking and antisocial rule-breaking.

Past research shows that prosocial rule-breaking is driven by prosocial intentions, empathy, and an inclination towards emotional guilt, whereas antisocial rule-breaking is inversely predicted by these factors (Hennigan & Cohn, 2022). While this illustrates differing motivations across moral dimensions, the studies presented in this dissertation are the first to show that lower legal reasoning and higher moral reasoning lead to greater prosocial rule-breaking. This differs from antisocial rule-breaking, which less influenced by moral reasoning but is instead indirectly suppressed by legal reasoning through the mediating effect of attitudes towards rules – a finding consistent with prior legal socialization research (Cohn et al., 2010; Cohn et al., 2012).

The integrated cognitive legal socialization model sets the cognitive processes of moral and legal reasoning as predictors of individuals' attitudes towards rules which in turn predicts rule-violating behavior (Cohn et al., 2010; Cohn et al., 2012, Cole et al., 2021). The research presented here extends these findings and establishes that prosocial rule-breaking is more directly influenced by these cognitive processes and this phenomenon may be better explained by deontological moral alignment and legal alignment than by more everyday measures of moral and legal reasoning (Shelton & McAdams, 1990; Cole et al., 2013; Cole et al., 2021). This adds to the growing body of legal socialization research by extending the integrated model beyond its classic foundations.

Previously, the integrated model has been based on Kohlbergian stage theory (Kohlberg, 1961; Tapp & Kohlberg, 1977), which has since been supplemented by important developments in moral reasoning research. While incorporating measures of everyday reasoning into the integrated model has been a step forward, the present studies provide an alternative approach to moral and legal reasoning by incorporating a new measure of moral and legal alignment based on the deontological coherence framework (Forsyth, 2020; Holyoak & Powell, 2016; Lee & Holyoak, 2020). The choice of naming these terms "alignment" rather than "reasoning" has added benefits beyond distinguishing them from other components of the reasoning process. The idea that we have an internally held moral and legal alignment provides a much-needed nuance in understanding the growing legal socialization literature on normative alignment (Jackson et al., 2012a, 2012b; Sun et al., 2018; Tyler & Jackson, 2018). The terms normative alignment and moral alignment have been used interchangeably to refer to the degree an individual's internally held moral values match with those of the law and the social order at large. This is an important topic because if an individual believes there is a mismatch between their internal moral values and normative legal values, they are more likely to engage in a wide range of rule-violating behavior (Tyler & Jackson, 2018; Jackson et al., 2012a). However, existing scales only focus on the belief in the mismatch of values without examining what those internally held values are (e.g., Jackson et al., 2012a).

For this reason, it is important to tease apart the idea of moral/normative alignment into the separate dimensions of moral alignment (alignment to internally held personal rules about helping) and legal alignment (alignment to the normative principles of authority and adherence to the established social order). By examining alignment to moral principles of altruistic helping for its own sake and alignment to the legal principles of authority, researchers may gain greater insight into normative alignment and increased utility when predicting rule-violating behavior. These internally held deontological rules about morality and the law may serve as the basis for those very values of which are mismatched to begin with. By integrating the recent research into normative alignment into the deontological moral and legal reasoning framework, we may add greater nuance and understanding about where such values are actually aligned. The expansion of the integrated model to include moral and legal alignment is just one step in this direction of greater nuance and predictive utility.

For example, previous scales that measure the single dimension of belief in the mismatch of values can only predict general rule-violating behavior (e.g., Jackson et al., 2012a) but lack the nuance needed to predict different types of rule-violating behavior such as prosocial rule-breaking. Studies 1 and 2 of this dissertation show that conceptualizing moral alignment and legal alignment as two separate dimensions provides this much needed ability. High moral alignment and low legal alignment predicts prosocial rule-breaking but not antisocial rule-breaking. Conversely, low moral alignment and low legal alignment predict antisocial rule-breaking but not prosocial rule-breaking. Intriguingly, the LAMAS scale and the expanded integrated model opens up an avenue to explain prosocial and antisocial rule-following behavior in addition to rule-breaking in a way that existing models cannot. An antisocial rule-follower (such as a willing Nazi soldier, or a police officer who eagerly enforces systemically racist laws) may be predicted by low moral alignment and high legal alignment.

The finding that the procedural justice model similarly predicts prosocial rule-breaking through the mediating effect of legitimacy as it does general rule-breaking (e.g., Trinkner & Cohn, 2014) has serious implications in the role the police have played in triggering the rise of many anti-authoritarian movements throughout history, including the recent Black Lives Matter protests. The procedural justice legal socialization model advocates that individuals' perception of the fairness of law enforcement agents (such as the police) is a crucial component in shaping people's attitudes towards obedience and disobedience of rules, laws, and societal norms (Fagan & Tyler, 2005; Fagan & Piquero, 2007; Piquero et al., 2005; Trinkner & Cohn, 2014; Tyler & Trinkner, 2017). This has significant implications for policy, practice, and future research. In addition to existing procedural justice research, the results from Study 3 point to the necessity of ensuring fairness in police operations as a means of promoting their legitimacy and bringing the rule of law in line with the moral values of the public.

When the police treat citizens poorly, they may be viewed as an illegitimate authority justifying a wide range of prosocial rule-violating behaviors. In the most extreme cases, such as the murder of George Floyd, this could trigger nation wide protests where many morally motivated citizens engage in prosocial rule-violating behavior for the sake of the greater good. Consistent with findings from previous legal socialization research, the results from this dissertation highlight the need for law enforcement agencies to prioritize procedural justice in their dealings with the public to foster a sense of legitimacy (Fagan & Tyler, 2005; Trinkner & Cohn, 2014; Tyler & Trinkner, 2017). This call for increased fairness is especially pressing considering the recent hostilities between the police and their treatment of peaceful protesters.

A significant number of individuals participating in peaceful protests advocating for the Black Lives Matter movement were arrested for nonviolent infractions (Hale et al., 2020; Snow, 2020). A considerable portion of these prosocial rule-breakers faced punishment under the "Civil Obedience Act" (1968), originally enacted in the 1960s to counteract civil rights activists inspired by Martin Luther King, Jr. (Gerstein, 2021). Senator Russell Long, a public proponent of racial segregation and critic of King, was instrumental in the law's creation. Interestingly, this legislation, initially aimed at undermining the civil rights movement, has recently been utilized to prosecute BLM activists (Gerstein, 2021).

Contrary to the belief that legal constraints on peaceful protests are a relic of the past and headed for prompt extinction, there has been a resurgence of in the enactment of such laws. Following the BLM protests, 36 laws curtailing the right to protest have been established in the United States, with another 44 proposed (International Center for Non-Profit Law, 2022). The United Nations Office of the High Commissioner for Human Rights has criticized this recent surge in legal constraints on peaceful assembly. These experts are particularly alarmed by the vaguely defined offenses and severe penalties (Day et al., 2021). Despite UN appeals to all U.S. states to halt anti-protest legislation and address police brutality, these laws persist, with many still undergoing legislative review (Day et al., 2021; International Center for Non-Profit Law, 2022). As sanctions and legal constraints on activism increase, ordinary citizens may grow more hesitant to engage in activism, considering the rising legal risks. It may fall on prosocial rule-breakers, who have historically advanced human rights and driven positive social change by challenging these laws.

Limitations and Future Directions

The current dissertation is not without limitations. For example, the samples used in these studies were primarily White (92.2% in Study 1, 80.4% in Study 2, and 68% in Study 3), and the sample used in Study 1 was primarily female (79.9%). This could have implications for the generalizability of the results of these studies. Members of different racial groups may have different levels of prosocial rule-breaking. For example, it is possible that Black Americans could score higher on prosocial rule-breaking likelihood because of a history of negative interactions with police and other authority figures. Highly prosocial Black Americans could potentially view these authority figures as less procedurally just and less legitimate which would influence their prosocial rule-breaking scores. Ensuring that future studies have an inclusive sample pool with a wide reaching demographic range would improve accuracy of future findings rather than relying on samples of mostly White participants.

Another limitation is the inherent subjective nature of morality and prosociality. Researchers are not immune to this subjectivity and our personal biases may frame the research questions we ask and the measurements that we use. For example the use of Wolpin's (1983) Delinquency Component of the National Youth Longitudinal Survey may not be the best choice as the scale was originally intended to capture more antisocial types of rule-breaking such as physical aggression. Choosing this scale because of its past use in legal socialization research and adapting it to measure prosocial rule-violating behavior may have unintended consequences. One of these may be capturing a more "aggressive" type of prosocial rule-breaking where one feels morally justified to attack others if they believe it is helping people. This could lead to misguided intervention programs where aggression is preserved under the impression it is helpful when it may cause more harm than good.

This subjective nature and potential harm of prosocial rule-breaking extends to scenarios used in the prosocial and antisocial rule-breaking scale used in all three of the studies in this dissertation. One such scenario of the PARB scale is executing an illegal U-turn to help a friend make it to a job interview on time. Regardless of the good intentions, the risk posed to the lives of passengers and other drivers should be considered seriously. The prosocial and antisocial rule-breaking (PARB) scale is measuring just one of several ways that prosocial rule-breaking can be conceptualized. This is not necessarily the end-all be-all definition of prosocial rule-breaking.

For example, in the industrial-organization literature, prosocial rule-breaking is defined as any instance where an employee intentionally violates a formal organizational policy, regulation, or prohibition with the primary intention of promoting the welfare of the organization or one of its stakeholders (Dahling, Chau, Mayer, 2012; Morrison, 2006). While this is a very specific definition, it is very different from the broad idea of breaking any rule with the intent to benefit of others as defined in the current dissertation.

While it's certainly worth acknowledging that rule-breaking with prosocial intent can be a force for positive social change, it is not necessarily beneficial to society and can potentially result in substantial harm despite being morally driven. Morality is subjective, varying among individuals in terms of what they consider the greater good and the best way to achieve it. For example, what counts as "prosocial" or "moral" varies greatly across the political spectrum. Someone with liberal ideals may find it prosocial to protect a woman's right to choose while someone with conservative ideals may find it prosocial to protect an unborn fetus' right to life.

Some of the most heinous acts committed in the United States and elsewhere were done so by individuals who believed they were morally justified. One instance is the Oklahoma City bombing by Timothy McVeigh, who saw his act as a valid defense of individual rights of all United States citizens (Herbeck & Michel, 2001). Furthermore, parents who mistakenly associate vaccines with autism may refuse mandatory vaccinations for their children, thereby putting them at risk of serious illnesses (Plotkin et al., 2009).

These subjective differences should absolutely be considered before implementing any measure or informing any real world program under the naive pretense that the intent to help others necessarily leads to helpful consequences. Deciding which acts of rule-breaking are morally justified is a philosophical question but research on the prosocial intent underlying such behaviors still serves to help us understand and predict a wide range of important behaviors regardless of their intended consequences.

Conclusions

Rule-breaking is often assumed to be antisocial in nature. While the harm caused by some instances of rule-breaking can be perceived as consequentially antisocial, little attention has been brought to the potential prosocial intentions underlying such acts. The main purpose of this dissertation was to determine the developmental factors leading one to become a prosocial rule-breaker. The studies presented in this dissertation aimed to detect differences between prosocial and antisocial rule-breaking in their developmental factors using the Integrated Cognitive Legal Socialization Model and the Procedural Justice Legal Socialization Model.

In order to better understand the multidimensional cognitive factors underlying the development of prosocial rule-breaking, I first created the Legal and Moral Alignment Scale based on the deontological coherence framework. Studies 1 and 2 detailed the development and validation of the legal alignment and moral alignment factors. Study 2 used these factors in the Integrated Cognitive Legal Socialization Model in place of the everyday legal and everyday moral reasoning scales typically employed as the two main predictors. The results showed that, generally, moral alignment positively associated with prosocial rule-breaking but negatively associated with antisocial rule-breaking while legal alignment either indirectly or negatively associated with both types of rule-breaking. Study 3 showed general consistency of these findings in a longitudinal study from late adolescence to adulthood. Study 3 also tested the procedural justice model longitudinally and found that perceptions of police fairness predict belief in police as legitimate authority figures which predicts prosocial rule-breaking, demonstrating consistency with prior legal socialization research.

These studies show that the integrated model is better at distinguishing between prosocial rule-breaking and antisocial rule-breaking due to its moral reasoning and legal reasoning factors. These results help make informed real world decisions on the factors that lead one to become a prosocial rule-breaker as opposed to an antisocial rule-breaker. While these findings can be used to inform intervention programs, forensic investigators, and psychologists wishing to understand the behavior of this unique class of rule-breakers, caution must be taken in making clear distinctions between prosocial intent and prosocial consequences as both are subjective and not necessarily one and the same.

www.ingramcontent.com/pod-product-compliance
Lightning Source LLC
LaVergne TN
LVHW020429080526
838202LV00055B/5089